Emergence
Of
The 'Me' Enterprise

Emergence
Of
The 'Me' Enterprise

A Blueprint for
Leadership in the 21st Century

Ashok B. Shah & G. Ross Kelly

Published by Gatekeeper Press
3971 Hoover Rd. Suite 77
Columbus, OH 43123-2839

ISBN: 9781619845091
eISBN: 9781619845107

Printed in the United States of America

1st Edition

This book is dedicated to the memory of our parents, to our families, and to our friends, colleagues, bosses and employees with whom we have worked. All contributed so much to each of us and our careers, and asked so little in return.

Contents

Foreword... ix

Part I: The New Reality

Chapter 1: Am I at Risk? 3

Chapter 2: The New Reality: The Changing Corporation 9

Chapter 3: A New Paradigm of Leadership............................ 29

Chapter 4: Am I Prepared? 43

Part II: The "Me" Enterprise

Chapter 5: The Emergence of the "Me" Enterprise.................. 49

Chapter 6: A Blueprint for the "Me" Enterprise..................... 59

       Mission.. 63

       Guiding Principles and Values............................... 70

       Deliverables 112

       Investment 124

       Promoting... 136

       Outcomes... 169

Part III: The Role of the Corporation

Chapter 7: The Silent Killers of Corporate Productivity
(and Individual Careers)... 175

Chapter 8: The Opportunity: The Corporation and
the "Me" Enterprise 199

Epilogue... 231

About the Book.. 235

About the Authors... 237

Foreword

WE BEGAN OUR careers in the field of information technology when the industry was in its infancy. From punch cards and clunky huge mainframes the size of gymnasiums, to nanotechnologies and wearables barely visible to the naked eye, we weren't driving the bus, but we were on the bus, in an industry that has, and continues to transform the world.

We have each spanned the corporate spectrum, from entry level, to "C" level, from start-ups to Fortune 50 corporations; through mergers, acquisitions and divestitures; through booming successes and colossal failures.

Over the past forty years, we have collaborated as teammates and as partners, in many countries and in many cultures. We've learned from and led teams that needed and sought our guidance, and teams that provided us guidance. We've had the opportunity to observe, to offer and share opinions, to ponder and reflect on new ideas and new technologies, to prognosticate and to draw conclusions.

Through a combined 80+ years of living and working in the world of technology, we continue to marvel at this wonderland of a revolution and the impact it is having on its creators, its users and the world that continues to be transformed as a result.

We marvel at the extraordinary ways in which technology has impacted us and the world around us. We also marvel at how technology has impacted the workplace, and in particular, leadership in the workplace.

It is difficult to draw conclusions or see patterns in the midst of a revolution. There is an expression that says, "You don't fully understand the instructions until after the bicycle has been put together." And though this technological revolution is far from over, patterns have begun to emerge . . . patterns that have worked to help leaders achieve success in the past, and more importantly, what is required to achieve success going forward.

We have enjoyed successes in our own careers, and we have worked for and with visionaries, entrepreneurs and leadership gurus who have enjoyed successes far greater than our own. Additionally, we've had discussions with hundreds of other leaders who have enjoyed similar successes. All cite the same patterns, the same themes, the same attitudes and attributes of what is required to succeed as a leader in a workplace that is increasingly dominated by technology, more global, more virtual, and more competitive, and changing at a pace that is unprecedented.

While neither we nor any of the individuals we have engaged with in this endeavor profess to have completely cracked the code on leadership success in this brave new world, the patterns of what it takes to succeed seem to be consistent. Today's leader is one who is more entrepreneurial, more assertive and more in charge of their own careers and their own results. They possess an array of skills, attitudes and values we have collectively come to define as the "Me" Enterprise.

Additionally, similar to the way an architect would devise a plan from a collection of ideas and visualizations, we have organized those attributes into the fashion of a blueprint . . . a blueprint for developing, constructing and sustaining the "Me" Enterprise.

While we have authored other books and publications on other topics in other genres, we do not present these findings as authors, as much as we present them as leaders and students of leadership. This publication represents a synthesis of views about how the role of leadership has evolved and how we believe it will continue to evolve in the 21st century; and the skills, characteristics and attributes that will separate the successful from the less successful. This book examines the phenomenon of "digitization" in the workplace. But more importantly, it examines the impact digitization has created for employees and leaders in that workplace, and the implications and challenges for those workers and leaders going forward.

It takes an analytical view of how the role of leaders has changed in a world that is more technical, more dynamic, more competitive and faster paced than ever before. Herein, we put forth a collection of ideas, attributes and practices that we believe to be essential to surviving and thriving in that new environment.

This book is written as a compilation of learnings we have collected from our own experiences and the experiences of others over the past forty years, with the intent of forging those learnings into a blueprint for how leaders flourish in their own careers, and how they train, mold, shape and lead their employees to succeed as well.

It is written for both current and aspiring leaders in large companies and small, who are first level supervisors, mid-level managers and senior executives and who are determined to excel in an increasingly competitive environment.

It is also written to pay tribute to the many individuals who molded and shaped our careers over the past forty years, be they our bosses, our colleagues or those who we were privileged to lead, as well as our customers and partners. They were our teachers. They are the ones who were instrumental in whatever successes we enjoyed, and whose fingerprints are embedded in the lessons put forth in this book.

Finally, it is written to convey a deep and profound expression of gratitude to our families. It was they who endured the endless travel, the international relocations, the many end-of-quarter or end-of-year stresses dominated by sleepless nights and ill tempers.

Emergence of the "Me" Enterprise" is our attempt to give back, to all who shaped us, molded us, taught us, were patient enough to follow us, and loved us enough to endure us. It is our hope that you will draw from it a fraction of the many lessons that we were fortunate enough to learn.

Welcome to the "Me" Enterprise.

Ashok B. Shah
G. Ross Kelly

PART I

The New Reality

"What happened to the nice, cozy, family oriented company that I used to know and love?"

Chapter 1

Am I at Risk?

The Monday Morning Surprise

IMAGINE THIS SCENARIO – You've been with your company for four years. When you were hired into your leadership position, you were told you would be on the "fast track." Your performance reviews have consistently been described as "exceeding expectations." You and your spouse just recently enjoyed a company paid cruise as a reward for the work you and your team did in getting a new product out the door to a demanding customer. You're a veteran of the downsizing wars, so you are not naïve to the realities of corporate life. But, so far, you have been spared any such fate, in large part because of your performance, and in part because of the success of your company and your division.

As you wind down your weekend on a Sunday evening, you make one last cursory check of your email before retiring for the evening. You see an email from your boss addressed to "All Managers," that reads: "Mandatory Meeting, Monday Morning, 9:00 am." This is not the first time your boss has called a last minute mandatory meeting, so you are not overly concerned. But the title of the email stays with you as you try to sleep.

The next morning, as you gather with the other members of the leadership team in the conference room, everyone is asking the same question, "Do you know what this is about?" But no one has an answer. Your boss walks in with a sober look on his face.

"I've called you here to announce something some of you may have suspected, but I could not talk about until now. Our company just announced that our division has been sold. I do not yet know what this will mean for any of us. The next three to four weeks will be devoted to analyzing our team's skills and capabilities and determining how they will fit in with the new company. All changes should be finalized within a month.

I know this is catching you by surprise, the same way it did me. Over the course of the day, there will be communications with each of your employees, and I will meet with each one of you to discuss what this could mean in more specific terms for you and your teams, and what you will need to do to get you and your team prepared. I'm sorry I don't have any more information to provide you at this time. . . ."

Monday morning surprise meetings are happening at an increasing rate. In small, mid-sized and large companies, these meetings appear to be happening with slightly different announcements, but they are all being driven by the same reasons, and all result in the same question . . . "How do I survive in this increasingly competitive and changing landscape?"

"We've been sold . . ."

"We will have to shut down . . ."

"We are merging . . ."

"Our division is being consolidated . . ."

"We are reorganizing . . ."

"We are acquiring/being acquired. . . ."

"We are offshoring our operations . . ."

As you return to your office, a hundred questions race through your mind . . .

What does this mean for me?

Will I have to leave the company?

If I'm offered a lesser position as an individual contributor, are my technical skills up to date?

Who do I know in other companies?

How current is my network outside my company?

Do I have my resume updated?

What if relocation is required with a new position? What would this mean for my family?

What is the state of the job market for my skills? Would I even be competitive in the marketplace?

Have I been complacent about staying current with my skills and what is going on in the marketplace?

Have I maintained my technical skills?

What about my employees? Have I adequately prepared them for this possibility?

Am I at risk?

Am I prepared?

The rate and pace of mergers, acquisitions, takeovers, makeovers and restructurings has intensified in dramatic fashion in the past twenty years, and with it, a transition to a new paradigm. The last remnants of the traditional, hierarchical approach to leadership and management are vanishing from the workplace at an accelerated rate, as are the benevolent attitudes and practices which companies once bestowed upon their employees.

Management methods that originated in the early 20th century which enabled the concept of mass production and fueled the greatest period of productivity in the history of man, are all changing, as are the social contracts that once existed between employer and employee.

The implicit understanding between employer and employee that once promised a salary, benefits, job security and the opportunity to build a lasting and productive career and safety net for families is still desired, but becoming increasingly difficult to keep. The thirty-year career, pension and finally the gold watch that our parents and grandparents worked diligently to earn by obediently abiding the corporate structure now seem to reside in the same archives as dial-up Internet access.

Corporations are challenged like never before to remain competitive, to remain profitable, and in many cases, to remain in business. As a result, nothing is constant, and no one is immune from the changes and consequences that come with these efforts. Employees, managers and leaders alike are at risk every day of losing their jobs, being demoted, being reassigned or getting lost in the churn of economic upheavals and competitiveness of their company.

In today's workplace, unlike politicians who are reelected to their offices every two, four, or six years, employees are analyzed and voted on every day. Regardless of position or title, every employee's performance and even the relevance of their job is under constant scrutiny as their companies continue to search for the magic formula that will reduce costs, generate greater revenues, improve margins, create a stronger competitive position in the marketplace, and in many cases, ensure the survival of the organization.

Employees must prove their worth every day, and learn to survive and thrive in an environment that offers fewer protections, and even fewer certainties.

Welcome to the new reality. . . .

Chapter 2

The New Reality:
The Changing Corporation

"There is no customer loyalty that two cents off can'tcure"

—Frank W. Woolworth,
Founder Woolworth "Five and Dime"

THE INTERNET EMERGED in the 1990's as a powerful new engine for commerce, triggering a seismic shift in how businesses operated. Revolutionary technologies spawned unprecedented improvements and efficiencies and dramatically transformed the way businesses executed financial transactions, telecommunications, manufacturing operations and business processes.

What became known as the "dot.com boom" was the trigger for some of the greatest innovations in the history of industry. New companies sprang up virtually overnight, offering a newer and better mousetrap, only to be surpassed by a newer and more improved device the following week. Innovators were catapulted from their garages to billionaire status with the flicker of an idea, and investors scrambled to fund the next IBM, Microsoft,

Google, Facebook or Apple that would generate 1000 x returns. As each new generation of technologies splashed onto the marketplace, the next generation was not far behind, ready to surpass and leave its predecessor in the dust.

There is an often quoted parable about a frog placed in a pot of boiling water. As the frog is placed in the boiling water, he immediately senses danger and jumps out. But when the frog is placed in a pot of water that is room temperature and the heat is gradually increased, he doesn't sense the danger until it is too late. As in the story of the frog, the changes that have driven the creation of these new corporate employment practices didn't happen overnight, nor or they the result of a singular force. Rather, they are a result of a confluence of factors that have been trickling into the workplace since the origins of the dot.com era.

For many employees and many companies, the pot has begun to boil . . .

Local to Global . . .

Technology has been the major force behind the changes that are driving new business practices, but it is not the sole driver. Other factors have contributed as well. One of these was the emergence of a global economy. Companies that once competed only within their national boundaries, and in some cases, in their own region, were suddenly thrust into an environment where they competed with lower cost providers across the globe. Technology enabled the creation of the global economy, but did little to prepare businesses to effectively compete in the new unbounded environment.

Corporations that once enjoyed a comfortable niche for their products and services, found themselves competing, almost without warning, with companies that offered comparable products of comparable quality, but at significantly lower prices. The emergence of the global economy not only altered the landscape of competition, it forced companies to re-think their entire business and workforce models.

Economic downturns, Cost Cutting and the search for the new norm . . .

An additional factor was the financial impact resulting from the disaster of 9/11, and the economic downturn of 2008. Those events further forced companies, large and small, to examine every operational and financial aspect of their business, to squeeze out every dollar of costs and reduce services to those that were essential to their survival.

Fairly or unfairly, the actions many corporations undertook to survive and sustain their profitability during these times, fostered a perception that they were focused only on their bottom line with little or no regard for the impact their actions would have on their employees, or their customers. The business world came to be viewed as doing anything and everything necessary to squeeze out every dollar of costs, regardless of the collateral damage or the debris left behind. Corporate reputations began to rival those of politicians and used car salesmen. The new operating norm for corporations toward customers and employees was viewed as "offer less for more." The reality is they had no choice if they were to survive.

The information age was spawned over thirty years ago, and shows no signs of slowing down. If anything, it continues to gain momentum, like the snowfall that began at the top of a mountain and created an avalanche as it continued downhill. As the pace of innovation continues to accelerate, business cycles continue to shrink, and windows of opportunity for companies to adapt and remain competitive open and close just as rapidly.

While corporations continue to take a public relations beating for reductions in services, benefits and other cost cutting measures, the reality is they could no longer compete with their traditional employment practices and cost models, given the demands of the new global economy. The days of the company car, unlimited expense accounts and lucrative pension plans in most companies have become a thing of the past. Leaders, who grew up and were accustomed to those more traditional corporate models and practices, have been left ill prepared and out of sync with the conditions of the new millennium. As a result, they now scramble to find ways to remain competitive, relevant . . . and employed.

Today's workforce paradigm is a far cry from that of the 1990s, or even the decade of the 2000s.

What were once absolutes are now uncertainties . . .

What once was vertical is now horizontal . . .

What was once fixed is now "agile" . . .

What once were jobs are now projects . . .

What once was job security are now job auditions . . .

What once was job satisfaction is now constructive dissatisfaction . . .

What once was seniority based, is now knowledge-based . . .

What once was clear and straightforward, is now fuzzy and complex . . .

What once were employees, are now contractors . . .

The dot.com era seems like a thousand years ago, yet its legacy is more powerful than ever. Competitive forces have never been greater and the mortality rate for companies and employees never higher. Five year plans have become 3 month plans. Companies remain in a constant state of reorganization, restructuring, consolidations, mergers and acquisitions.

And each change results in leadership teams and in some cases, entire workgroups being dissolved, scrambled and dispatched in the flicker of a Monday morning staff meeting.

Digitization of the Industrial World

Companies are now almost entirely driven by software innovations, either as developers or consumers of technology, and all are challenged to incorporate the latest innovation into their business model, to remain relevant, and more importantly, solvent.

General Electric, one of the icons of the industrial age, is a classic example of a corporate transformation to the new "digitized" world. Jeff Immelt, Chairman and CEO of the corporate industrial giant, shared his perspective in an interview with McKinsey's Rik Kirkland:

> We think about this as digitization of the industrial world. We as a company didn't go to bed one night and say, "We can't be an industrial company anymore. We need to be more like Oracle. We need to be more like Microsoft. It happened more on an evolutionary basis, really based on the industries we're in and the technology we serve. So, industrial companies are in the information business whether they want to be or not. I took over an industrial company. Now, it will be known as an analytics company.

Traditionally known for light bulbs, turbine engines and other large industrial products, GE currently monitors and analyzes 50 million data elements from 10 million sensors on

$1 trillion of managed assets daily to move customers toward zero unplanned downtime.

The company is selling off its division that makes refrigerators and microwave ovens, and now concentrates on electric power generators, jet engines, locomotives, and oil-refining gear. Further, it has made a significant bet on developing software to connect these devices to the Internet. There's a term for this trend of adding network connections to hardware other than computers: "the Internet of Things." GE believes its opportunity lies in what it calls the "Internet of Really Big Things."

In the past five years, GE has hired hundreds of software developers, created its own operating system, and fashioned dozens of applications that it says will make planes fly more efficiently, extend the life of power generators, and allow trains to run faster. GE's plan is to sell this software to other manufacturers of Really Big Industrial Things, and to be a top 10 software company by 2020. That is an ambitious transformation, which would put GE in the same category as a software company as Microsoft, IBM, and Oracle, an ambition that some analysts have difficulty swallowing.

In support of the company's transformation, it has launched a marketing campaign and television advertising series to attract the top software engineers and technologists to help "digitize" itself in order to remain relevant in today's marketplace.

But what has that transformation meant to the thousands of GE employees and leaders in the company's more traditional lines of business who have been forced to re-engineer their own careers to remain relevant and employed through that transition? To what extent were they prepared to adapt their own careers given the company's new vision and new direction?

The Evolving Digitized Corporation

Digitization has forced companies into a new realm. While those companies are as diverse as the businesses and industries in which they reside, they are all confronted with the same emerging characteristics, trends and core beliefs that have come to dictate their success in the "digitized" world.

Consider the following trends:

- Companies continue to be increasingly global, and increasingly virtual.

    Globalization today has reached a maturity level which is simply a fact of corporate life. American cars are made in Europe and Japan. European and Japanese cars are made in the United States. Products are designed in one company, manufactured in another, and sold in yet another. Companies large and small are engaged with partners, suppliers and customers outside their national border and that trend will only continue.

    The same can be said of virtualization. Employees spend more time today on conference calls and webinars than they do in face-to-face meetings. Team members reside in different locations, work in different locations, and in many cases have never met many of their teammates face-to-face. As virtual reality technology becomes more sophisticated and more affordable, it will become even more commonplace.

- Companies are in a constant state of transition and metamorphosis . . .

    Today's business mantra increasingly seems to be, "There is no business that cannot be improved through a merger, an acquisition, or a re-structuring. And if that doesn't work, do it again!" Businesses are in a constant state of transformation and evolution. No product is permanent; no business unit is permanent; no business model is permanent; no organizational structure is permanent, and no company is permanent. Transition is to businesses what the appetite is to the human body . . . constant, and always looking for more. With a frequency that seems only to increase, companies, like the amoeba, are always taking a new shape, morphing into the strategy of the month.

- Companies are increasingly "digitized."

As Robert Terceck asks so poignantly in his book, *Vaporized*, "What will your business look like in a world increasingly defined by software?" As the term "digitization" implies, software and technology now dominate the business world, and those companies that are making the transformation to a digitized economy remain relevant. Those that are excelling in that world are considered "intensely" digitized. In these corporations, technology is embraced as a top-to-bottom business strategy, and is at the core of the corporation's culture and mission.

- Companies are increasingly complex . . .

Corporations are increasingly complex, and will become even more so. That complexity is due in part to the constant wave after wave of new technologies, and in part to the growing virtual nature of its day-to-day activities. A third and perhaps even greater element of complexity consists of the continuous introduction and changes in new products, new strategies, new focus, new initiatives, and new business models, all in a constant pursuit of growth and profitability. The once time-honored axiom, "Stability is the enabler of success," has gone the way of the rotary telephone.

- Companies are increasingly ambiguous . . .

As business strategies and objectives change at an increasing rate, as new initiatives are launched, as new business rules and policies are adapted, as shared responsibilities are bestowed, as cross-functional and cross-organizational projects are launched, questions of responsibility and authority arise, and fewer and fewer of these questions are answered with certainty. When asked about his responsibilities, one high tech executive told an interviewer, "We live in a constant state of ambiguity." Who has the ultimate authority? Who is accountable? Who approves resources, budgets? Who allocates funds? Who has final approval? Ambiguity is an increasing characteristic of the digitized environment, with less and less time or attention devoted to what are sometimes considered the "minute details" of making things happen, such as:

- Who is "Responsible?"
- Who is the "Approver?"
- Who provides "Support?"
- Who is to be "Consulted?"
- Who is to be "Informed?"

More and more frequently these shared responsibilities are not documented in detail in the digitized corporation, but are more often "inferred," with the individuals left to work the details themselves.

- Companies endure an increasing maze of Regulations . . .

There are financial regulations that any corporation must adhere to, referenced by documents referred to as "GAAP" Standards (Generally Accepted Financial Principles). Public corporations have increasingly lengthy and detailed financial regulations, governed by the Federal Trade Commission, that they must adhere to. An increasing number of regulations are governed by the "Sarbanes-Oxley" legislation, which was enacted to counter corporate accounting scandals, such as Enron and WorldCom. And a growing list of environmental, cyber security, workforce, privacy and counter-terrorism regulations have become standard compliance requirements for corporations, in addition to the many state and local laws and regulations that must be complied with. The regulatory environment has increased dramatically in the past twenty years, and will continue to increase even more.

- Companies face increasing levels of activism among shareholders and stakeholders . . .

Corporate boards were once considered passive, "rubber stamp" approvers of corporate policies and strategies. That was until laws were passed that held them accountable for the actions of the Corporations they supposedly directed. Today, board members and directors have becoming increasingly active and engaged in the day-to-day operations of their companies. The same can be said of outside groups, such as shareholders, public policy activists, environmental groups, civil rights activists and local community leaders. This trend is expected to do nothing but continue in corporations, with leaders left in some cases to devote as much time and energy to managing external stakeholder interests as they do in managing internally.

- Companies endure a perpetual state of stress and tension . . .

The digitized corporation is one that is never at rest, and never satisfied. Whatever last quarter's results were, whatever last month's sales performance was, whatever has been achieved to date, must be exceeded in the coming months, the coming quarter or the coming year. Those who reside in public corporations continually hear from their leadership teams, "THIS is our most important quarter!" And leaders in all corporations hear, "I know we did better than ever last month/year; but it will mean nothing if we don't exceed that this month/year!"

Like the insatiable appetites of power hungry titans, the corporate environment is one of perpetual stress and tension, driven by the never-ending demands of "Whatever was accomplished yesterday, more must be accomplished today!"

The Evolving Corporation . . .

- *Maturing – Global, Virtual*
- *On the Edge – Transient*
- *Intense Digitization*
- *Increasingly Complex*
- *Always Morphing*
- *Increasingly Ambiguous*
- *Maze of Regulations*
- *Expanding Risks*
- *Growing Activism*
- *Perpetually Stressed*

"Digitization," "Uberization" and Disruptions

Digitization is transforming the way companies operate and in some cases, turning conventional business wisdom upside down. Corporations and their leaders remain in a constant state of re-inventing their business models as they try to keep pace with the rapidity of technological innovations and the competitive landscape those innovations create. But technological innovations are demonstrating the potential to do much more than redefine business models . . . they are creating the capacity to bring them to extinction.

Some analysts call the emergence of software the "4th Industrial Revolution," or the "Exponential Age," an age in which many companies and industries will soon be disrupted, if not eliminated. Analysts see a future which will dramatically alter, if not eradicate many jobs and companies, citing rapidly emerging trends in artificial intelligence, health, autonomous and electric cars, education, 3D printing and agriculture. Beyond the challenges of adopting and integrating the latest technologies into their business model, businesses face an even greater potential for disruption – they could become extinct.

In a recent survey conducted by IBM, a group of senior executives were asked what worried them most about the future of their businesses and their careers. Getting "Uberized," having "Uber syndrome," or the process of "Uberization" were common phrases used to describe their biggest fear. In other words, they are most worried about getting disrupted, or worse, eliminated altogether by a digital upstart from outside their industry, the same way Uber has roiled the taxi industry.

The angst over getting struck by their industry's equivalent to Uber is, of course, not exactly new. Ever since Clayton Christensen wrote "The Innovator's Dilemma," CEOs have been looking over their shoulder for unexpected disruptive technologies that might upend their company. But the frequency with which it's happening, and the way in which the upstarts are reshaping whole industries rather than just slowly pushing out veteran players, is what keeps executives running scared. Companies are one innovation away from extinction, and their leaders know it all too well.

In 1998, Kodak had 170,000 employees and sold 85% of all photo paper worldwide. Within just a few years, the quality and costs of digital cameras completely disrupted Kodak's very existence. Though the company attempted to convert their business model to digital imaging, in 2012, with fewer than 7,000 employees remaining on their payroll, the company filed for bankruptcy.

This phenomenon of "Uberization," is described by John Kennedy, technology editor of the Silicon Republic, with the following paradoxical observations:

1. The world's largest taxi company (Uber) owns no taxis.

2. The world's largest accommodation provider (Airbnb) owns no real estate.

3. The largest communications companies (Skype, WhatsApp, Facebook Messenger and Viber) own no infrastructure.

4. The world's most valuable retailer (Alibaba) has no inventory.

5. The most popular media platform (Facebook) creates no content.

6. The fastest growing banks (Kickstarter, Apple Pay) actually have no money.

7. The world's largest movie house (Netflix) owns no cinemas.

8. The largest software vendors (Apple, Facebook, Google) don't write the apps.

Further, consider the case of Tesla in the automotive industry. The electric automobile manufacturer's founder and CEO, Elon Musk, has introduced a business model to sell his electric-powered automobiles directly to consumers, without the intermediate costs of the traditional automobile dealership. If he has his way, the automotive industry could become the next Uber. Many analysts see the sales model as just the tip of the iceberg for the automotive industry.

Analysts predict that the first self-driving cars will be available to the public as early as 2018. Around 2020, analysts predict, the complete industry will be disrupted. Instead of buying a car, individuals will be able to call a car with their phone, have it show up at their location and drive them to their destination. They will not need to park it. Automobiles will become our personal, automated chauffeur, escorting us to and from our destinations, on demand. In such a model, we will only pay for the driven distance, all while being productive during transport.

Is it possible that our children or grandchildren will never need a driver's license, or even own a car? What are the implications for businesses that today are completely reliant on the current automobile business model?

. . . for automobile manufacturers whose very existence relies on the premise that everybody wants their own car, using internal combustible engines?

. . . for cities that could have up to a 90% reduction in the need for parking spaces and garages? For the real estate developers who own those parking garages?

. . . for insurance companies when traffic accidents and fatalities are projected to be reduced by more than 85% with self-driving vehicles?

While traditional automobile companies are taking an evolutionary approach to building a better car, analysts say software companies, such as Google, Tesla and Apple are taking the revolutionary approach to completely disrupt the traditional market by creating a computer on wheels.

What other industries could be impacted by this type of disruption? If automated vehicles afford workers the ability to be as productive in a self-driven car as they are in their homes or their offices, where a worker lives could be less and less relevant. Traditionally, choices about where you live have been driven largely by where you work. What happens when workers are able to make choices about where they live, not based on the location of their company, but based on the quality of life they want for themselves and their families?

If workers can untether their decisions about where they live from the location of their workplace, what would that mean for the real estate and construction industry? If commuting to and from work were no longer an issue, would that mean fewer homes and developments clustered around large, crowded cities, and more construction and development in more rural, more desirable locations? What would that mean for municipalities as commercial land use and tax bases diminish at an even greater rate than they are doing today?

Electric vehicles are yet another potential blow to the fossil fuel industry, which is already suffering from the growing emergence of solar energy. Solar production has been on an exponential curve for 30 years, and its impact is now being felt. Last year, more solar energy was installed worldwide than fossil fuel-based energies. Electricity is becoming cheaper and cleaner, leaving some analysts to project that by the year 2025, all coal companies will be out of business, and the petroleum industry will be less than 1/3 of what it is today.

With cheap electricity comes cheap and abundant water. As scientists remind us, we do not have a scarce water problem, we have a scarce "drinking" water problem. Desalination now only needs 2k electricity per cubic meter of water. Imagine what would be possible if clean, cheap, abundant drinking water is available in virtually any location.

Manufacturing is another industry that is feeling the burn, primarily with the emergence of 3D printing technologies. Over the last ten years, the price of the cheapest 3D printer has come down from $18,000 to $400. In that same timespan, they have become 100 times faster. All major shoe companies have begun to use 3D printing to make their shoes. Airplane manufacturers are using 3D printers to create spare parts. The space station now has a printer that eliminates the need for the large amount of spare parts they used to have in the past.

At the end of this year, new smartphones will have 3D scanning possibilities.It is now possible to 3D scan your feet and print your own shoes at home. China has 3D printed a complete 6-story office building. It is estimated that by 2027, 10% of everything that's being produced will be 3D printed. What impact will 3D printing, as well as other technologies, have on the manufacturing industry? What impact will it have on workers whose livelihood is in the manufacturing industry?

Analysts predict that 70-80% of jobs that exist today will disappear in the next 20 years. Many will be replaced but with dramatically different skills required. Further, it is predicted that less than half the companies that exist today will be the employer for those jobs.

The "Uberization" of Management?

An adjunct to the concept of "Uberization," and another term recently added to the corporate lexicon, is the term, "disintermediation," which occurs when the "middle man," or the intermediary that stands between a product or a service and the consumer, is eliminated. Real estate brokers, manufacturers' representatives, automobile dealerships and retail stores are but a few examples of intermediaries. What does an employee, whose company and career are dependent on being an intermediary, do when that function has been eliminated? What does a company do when its very existence is that of an intermediary? What do automotive dealerships do if the Tesla sales model of selling directly to consumers begins to take off?

The concept of "Uberization" is not only happening to companies; they are happening inside of companies as well, typically in the form of "flattening the organization." One of the first areas companies look at when attempting to reduce costs and improve efficiencies is the prospect of reducing unnecessary layers of management. Organizational hierarchy charts that once had six or seven layers of management are being reduced to two or three. Removing layers of management, and in some cases, entire groups, are another form of disintermediation, which impacts individuals and leaders just as it does companies.

Where does the concept of the Uberization or disintermediation of a management structure end? How far can it go? Can an organization have only three levels of leadership and still effectively sell its products or services? Can it have only two? One? Is it possible that the entire leadership structure of an organization can be "Uberized?"

SumAll, a New York based marketing analytics start-up, thinks it is possible. The firm is experimenting with a concept in which they do not employ permanent leaders, but instead, allow employees to elect their leaders on a quarterly basis. The firm's CEO, Dane Atkinson, says the concept is not simply about costs, but the idea that employees know those within their ranks who are best positioned to lead, in many cases, identifying leaders who would otherwise be invisible in a more traditional corporate setting.

Zappos, an Amazon owned online shoe and clothing shop, employs what it calls a "holocracy," a concept that removes power from a management hierarchy and distributes it across clear roles. The idea is not to manage workers, but to manage "the work."

Similar to traditional companies such as Kodak, who could not have imagined that their business could become extinct, could traditional management roles be the next victim of Uberization?

What is a Leader to Do?

Today's technology driven climate has generated endless new ideas, new possibilities and new opportunities. It has yielded better products and services, faster cycle times, improved efficiencies and more precise performance and quality. Yet in doing so, it has created unprecedented challenges in which businesses and its leaders can be disrupted or rendered extinct in the blink of an eye. Corporations are being forced to address these challenges, all driven by the need to remain competitive, relevant and employed in the world of digitization.

The leaders and employees who are surviving and thriving in this new environment are doing so because they are adapting to changes that are equally dramatic. They are changing their approach to employment; they are changing their attitudes about how they manage their work and their careers, and they are changing their skill sets.

What are the profiles of leaders who are not only surviving in this increasingly competitive and demanding work environment, but excelling? What are the defining characteristics and traits of leaders whose careers are taking off, while others are stagnating? The following chapters will examine and define these qualities and lay out a blueprint for surviving and thriving in this era of digitization, Uberization and yet-to-be identified upcoming disruptions.

Chapter 3
A New Paradigm of Leadership

THE OBJECTIVES OF leadership . . . to organize, motivate, mobilize, inspire and accomplish . . . are timeless. They have remained unchanged since biblical times. However, the means by which to achieve those outcomes continue to evolve, change and adapt to the times and the environment in which they are applied.

In 2012, a study was published on behalf of the United Nations Global Compact and Principles for Responsible Management Education entitled, "Leadership in a Rapidly Changing World," which examined the evolutionary nature of leadership. The study described how leadership has evolved over the past century as business circumstances and economic models dictated:

- The "great man" of the pre-war era:

    This leader was charismatic, always male, possessing certain heroic leadership traits and natural abilities of power and influence that made him inherently superior and born to lead. These ideas about leadership were entirely in keeping with an era when there was a strong belief in genetic superiority - that men were inherently superior to women and people with white skin were inherently superior to others.

Think: Franklin Roosevelt.

- The "rational manager" of the 1950s and 1960"s:

This style of leadership involved directing and controlling others using an impersonal approach, rules and standardized procedures. Again, these were ideas about business leadership that fit their times. Post-war, organizations became much larger and more bureaucratized and ad hoc decision-making broke down. Thinking was dominated by faith in the power of scientifically-grounded rational planning to break free from the limitations of emotion.

Think: Thomas Watson, IBM

- The "change agent" of the mid-70s and 1980s:

In this era, we began to think of effective leadership being all about how to lead change. This period saw the rise of leader as influencer, relying less on the formal authority of organizational hierarchy, and placing more emphasis on the role of interpersonal skills, team-working and team leadership. This way of thinking about leadership was called for by changing times. Ideas from the fields of psychology and the behavioral sciences began to have more influence on thinking about leadership, finding fertile ground in the wake of the first major recession in the post-war period as we moved from a stable business environment to one of constant change. Organizations needed to change and become more flexible. Outsourcing and subcontracting grew, and organizations moved from rigid hierarchies to matrix structures.

Think: Lee Iacocca, Chrysler

- The "relational leader" of the 1990's and 2000's:

  The period saw less focus on the individual, and more interest in how effective leadership emerged from the way groups of people work together, with more attention paid to emotional intelligence and understanding how networks work. The idea of objective truths gave way to reality being socially constructed. There was recognition that leadership is not confined to a select group of people occupying the boardroom, but emerges anywhere in the organization. Change was now recognized as the norm, placing increased emphasis on the leader's ability to continually learn in order to adapt, and to encourage the development and growth of others. Globalization encouraged a stronger focus on leading cross-culturally and, coupled with the information age, also led to increasing focus on how to lead complex virtual teams.

  Think: Steve Jobs.

- The "global citizen" of the 21st Century

  A decade into the 21st century, with shifting power structures in an increasingly globalized society, new roles are emerging for governments and businesses, and in turn, for leaders. Success is now measured in much broader terms than just profit and loss or narrowly focused metrics. Business leaders are being forced to adopt a broader definition of what counts as success and leading across conventional business boundaries.

  Think: Mark Zuckerberg, Elon Musk, Sheryl Sandberg

* * *

This evolutionary view of leadership serves as a context for examining and defining the attributes of the leader in the modern era, but more importantly, it unveils the challenges leaders face in recognizing and adapting to a new leadership style as circumstances and economic and social conditions change. Leaders in the 21st century must look far beyond profit and loss and operational excellence, as their measures of effectiveness. They must navigate the issues not just of a global economy bound by international governance laws, but also of a global culture, bound by societal laws of social justice. They must lead their businesses not just in financial terms, but in social terms, in issues of culture, language, environment, social consciousness and giving back.

Transition to the Knowledge Economy

This new and complex world of leadership is embodied in what many summarize as the transition from an industrial world to a digitized world . . . from an industrial based economy to what is referred to as the knowledge economy. This transition is especially complex today because different companies operate on either side of that spectrum, and in some cases, on the cusp of that transition, with practices and processes of both worlds. As a result, many of today's leaders are forced to navigate within an organizational climate with split personalities.

There are industrial-oriented companies that continue to employ traditional management practices born in the early days of the 20th century, and there are new and emerging companies that personify the knowledge economy and the cultural changes that have accompanied that new culture. This period of "living on the cusp" between the two approaches represents one of the biggest challenges leaders have faced since the study of leadership began, and many who have leadership roles today sit directly on that cusp, with one foot on the boat and the other on the dock.

Getting from here to there . . .

The authors of "Complexity Leadership Theory: Shifting from the industrial age to the knowledge era," published in the August 2007 issue of *Leadership Quarterly*, frame the challenge as such:

> "Leadership models of the last century have been products of top-down, bureaucratic paradigms. These models are eminently effective for an economy based on the premise of physical production, but are not well-suited for a more knowledge oriented economy."

While there are thousands of corporations and businesses in the world today, and while the world is rapidly migrating toward a knowledge-based economy, many companies continue to operate and employ leadership styles that are remnants of the "Industrial Age" paradigm. Most companies and leaders seem to be well aware of the changes happening around them. They seem to know there is a "there" out there, but struggle with how to define exactly what "there" is, and how to get from "here" to "there."

Our efforts to examine this dilemma began with an exercise designed first to define the broad and diverse landscape of the businesses and corporations in which leaders find themselves.

The Diverse Corporate Landscape: On the Spectrum from "Structured to Fuzzy"

Corporations and businesses are as unique as the individuals that run them. From the traditional, industrial type manufacturing companies, to the latest, glitziest, high-tech phenomenon, to the local "mom and pop" on the street corner, no two are exactly alike, and no two can be managed in exactly the same way. To begin our examination, let's frame the landscape in which those corporations reside on a spectrum we call "Structured" to "Fuzzy."

On one end of the spectrum, there are the more structured, "materials-oriented" businesses, consistent with the Industrial era leadership model. Those are organizations whose products and services are driven primarily by physical production, and tend to rely on a more traditional, top-down management style. From the manufacturing assembly plants of General Motors, to the logistics processing of the United Parcel Service (UPS) to the local lumberyard or cement production plant, the success of a "structured business" is its ability to manufacture or process physical materials as efficiently as possible, and most likely rely on a more traditional leadership style to achieve their objectives.

On the other end of the spectrum are companies that are more "software oriented" or knowledge-based companies. They are typically newer, more technology-oriented, more entrepreneurial, and operate in a more complex, distributed environment. Those corporations tend to employ a more flexible management style, and a culture that promotes business practices such as work-at-home, flexible hours and cross-functional teaming, hence their characterization as "fuzzy."

"Knowledge based" companies are typically less engaged in physical materials and more in intellectual decision-making. From software companies to hospitals to NASA, these enterprises rely on the "knowledge" of their workforce. They typically work with less structure in terms of time and location, and as a result, employ different methods of leadership, management and metrics.

Just as we appreciate the extraordinary successes the

industrial age has produced employing traditional, top-down management practices, it is our belief that many of those practices would be less effective in a more distributed, entrepreneurial, knowledge-based organization. The same can be true for the opposite scenario, which illustrates the challenges of leadership in today's workplace.

The corporate landscape today includes "structured" organizations, "fuzzy" organizations, "traditional" organizations, "entrepreneurial" organizations, and all those that fall somewhere in between those extremes. The individuals who have leadership responsibilities in these organizations face the challenge of finding the right balance of leadership styles and skills to match the organizational environment in which they are expected to lead. Success in one organizational environment does not necessarily guarantee success in another.

John Sculley was a highly successful CEO at PepsiCo, which could be characterized as a "structured/traditional" corporation. He was handpicked by Steve Jobs to become his successor at Apple (a "fuzzy/complex" organization), with the expectation that he would bring the same marketing prowess and business success to Apple that he achieved at PepsiCo.

In contrast to the success he enjoyed at PepsiCo, Sculley's tenure at Apple was pockmarked with missed opportunities, misaligned strategies, and tensions and disagreements with the company's founder which even led to Jobs' ouster from the company. After ten years of frustrations in the boardroom and in the marketplace, Sculley also was ousted.

There is an expression that says, "Where you stand depends on where you sit." The corollary to that expression goes one step further to say, "Where you land depends on how you fit."

Where would your leadership style best fit in the following graphic? What type of corporate culture best matches your skills, your temperament?

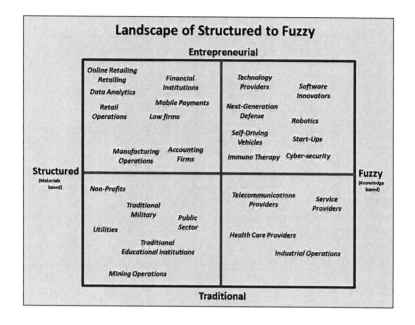

What is on the Horizon for Leaders in the 21st Century?

Where there were once clear, authoritative rules for managing, directing and leading, the new paradigm of leadership involves a wide array of scenarios and circumstances that leaders must navigate. Nowadays these rules are not quite as concrete, and in some cases, are still being negotiated.

For example:

- In many corporations, leaders may manage employees who are more knowledgeable than they are themselves. . . .

    In a traditional manufacturing environment, chances are the manager on the shop floor earned their position by virtue of performance and seniority, thus having more experience and presumably more knowledge than the workers he or she manages. Compare that to a physicist who works for NASA, or a physician who works in a hospital. The managers who supervise these individuals are most likely not physicists or physicians, but administrators. In these and many other "knowledge based" environments, the boss is challenged to manage employees who know their domains much better than the boss.

- Leaders must manage globally, virtually . . .

More and more corporations are becoming multi-national and global. Products are designed in one location, engineered in another location and may be manufactured in yet a third location. As a result, leaders are increasingly challenged to manage a workforce of multiple nationalities, multiple languages and different cultures. In many cases, managers and employees never meet face-to-face, but only virtually, via teleconferences, Skype or other virtual means. This represents a paradigm change for leaders. How do I effectively communicate? How do I create a virtual high performance team? How do I manage language/cultural differences? How do I remain visible?

- Leaders must acquire and assimilate talent on a just-in-time basis . . .

The rapidly increasing pace of business includes equally rapid changes in customer requirements, expectations and products. As product portfolios change, so do the needs for new skills and talent. Long-term loyalty of employees is transforming to "just in time" loyalties. Leaders are faced with the challenges of recruiting, training, orienting new talent on a just-in-time basis, and the questions that accompany those challenges . . . How do I attract new talent? How do I recruit? How do I incent and reward? How do I manage loyalties?

- Leaders are turning over at an unprecedented rate . . .

As mergers, acquisitions, reorganizations, portfolio destructions, and other product and organizational changes increase, so does the turnover of managers and leaders. Employees and work teams who once experienced a change in leadership once every 2-4 years, are now introduced to a new leader on average of every 6-9 months. These leaders, in turn, are expected to establish relationships, credibility, expectations and a new management style in a matter of weeks – and in some cases – days, and achieve results in the process. This is a paradigm change for leaders. How do I provide continuity to employees and customers? How do I survive and thrive?

- The cost of leadership has increased exponentially, raising increasing questions about their value . . .

In previous times of prosperity, leadership costs were masked by huge growth and profitability rates. Now with the new normal of lower growth rates, combined with escalating compensation levels, the cost of leadership has become much more visible and a growing concern. The leadership challenges have become increasingly significant. How do I reduce costs? How do I create value? Can I increase my span of leadership control to offset costs? How do I demonstrate my value so as not to call attention to my compensation?

- Leaders are on metrics overload . . .

One of the fastest growing sectors in the software driven, digitized economy is the area of business intelligence and analytics. Where we once had the capability to measure or monitor only major performance indicators, such as output, time and expense (i.e., "How long did it take?" "How much did it cost to produce?"), analytics software has now provided companies the ability to measure performance at micro-levels. On the surface, the ability to analyze and measure the finer nuances of performance may appear to contribute to increases in productivity. For its leaders, however, it could have the opposite effect.

The growing penchant for a corporation's desire to gather, analyze and report performance data not only adds significant costs, but in many cases, also robs leaders of their time and ability to lead.

- Leaders must succeed in a low growth/high expectations environment . . .

  Average growth rates in the 1990's were 3-4%. Today, those growth rates are closer to 1-2%. Leaders are living in a new, lower growth normal. However, the expectations of many investors and stakeholders have yet to adjust to the new realities. What was good enough yesterday is not good enough today.

  The leadership challenges . . . How do I credibly communicate the realities of the day? How do I remain competitive in this new environment? How do I remain relevant . . . today? Tomorrow? Even the very ratios of one leader for 8-10 employees are in question. Can this be 1 to 40? 1 to 100?

- Leaders are expected to manage within a climate of "High risk/High reward"

  Companies, in order to survive in an increasingly competitive environment, are assuming greater risks.

Their hope and expectations are (1) to survive and remain competitive, and (2), to realize higher rewards. Accordingly, these companies look for leaders willing to assume high risk/ high reward type opportunities and challenges. More and more companies are assuming the mantra, "Determined to succeed; but willing to risk failure in the process." They expect the same of their leaders.

- Leaders must continually remain current in their technical knowledge amidst a constant barrage of new data, new information, new software, new applications and new practices...

  With new technologies come new practices, new processes, and new knowledge requirements. Increasingly leaders are required to learn, assimilate and teach new practices, new processes and new technologies at an unprecedented rate. The leadership challenges... How do I continue to learn, both on my own and through the benefit of my employer at levels that keep me current and relevant? How do I find ways to learn on my own what my employer cannot or does not provide in terms of critical learning? And how do I teach my employees?

In the previous chapter, we described emerging trends that characterize the corporations of the 21st century, as being...

  ... Maturing ... more global; more virtual

  ... On the edge, transient

  ... Subject to intense digitization

  ... Increasingly complex

  ... Always morphing

... Increasingly ambiguous

... Involved with a maze of regulations

... Expanding risks

... Growing activism

... Perpetually stressed

In a similar vein, the challenge for today's leaders is to develop the skills and leadership styles to address these characteristics. Thus is the profile of the leader in the digitized economy.

The Evolving Leader of the 21st Century . . .

- *More Global*
- *More Virtual*
- *More Entrepreneurial*
- *Results Driven*
- *Transient*
- *Intensely Technology Driven*
- *In a state of perpetual learning and adapting*
- *Foster high risk / high reward behaviors*
- *Employees more knowledgeable than bosses*

* * *

The challenges for leaders today are numerous, complex and intensifying in the world of digitization and they are increasingly confronted with the following questions:

How do I survive and thrive in this ever-changing environment?

What are the characteristics, the attributes I must develop?

How do I develop those attributes and skills?

How do I teach them to those that I lead?

Am I prepared to lead in this era of digitization?

Chapter 4
Am I Prepared?

"Anything than can be vaporized, will be. Any part of a company's operation that can be turned into information, or replaced by software will be. That's a certainty."

—Robert Terceck

IN THE AFTERMATH of the Monday morning meeting in which you learned that the Division of the company where you are employed had just been sold, your mind was flooded with questions...

... Have I become complacent in my role with this company?

... Have I been lulled into an assumption that there was a natural career path for me within this company, thus ignoring the need to consider the prospects of changing jobs or companies?

... Have I become too casual or dismissive of the possibility that my job or my company could possibly go away?

. . . Have I been too dismissive of calls from headhunters pitching new opportunities to me?

. . . Have I become too involved in internal, administrative work so that my skills are no longer relevant or competitive?

. . . Do I still have the capability to compete in the open marketplace?

Your thoughts and emotions are flooded with questions, self-doubt and annoyance. You find that you have become too complacent with your current circumstances and have been left completely unprepared for the reality that just hit you.

Back at your desk, you researched the company that just acquired your Division. They were a company that 24 hours before was completely unknown to you, and now, they are your new prospective employer. You began to scroll your Rolodex, thumbing through the names and numbers of those headhunters you had so casually dismissed, and the names of colleagues and mentors that you have not spoken with in many months . . .

. . . Have I not kept up with them? And them with me?

. . . When is the last time I had lunch with my former boss who supported and mentored me over the years?

. . . What is the name of the CEO who told me to stay in touch?

For the first time since being a novice, first line manager, you felt perplexed about what to do next, knowing that whatever it was, it had to happen quickly.

There is a timeless truth that people are most vulnerable in their careers during times when they are employed and comfortable in their current position. During those times, complacency sets in. They do not give any thought to being prepared for their next opportunity. It's only when they sense the possibility of being displaced that they begin to think about alternatives. And then, in many cases, it's too late.

How many leaders today are convinced that their company, their division, their job could never be "Uberized?" How many leaders at Kodak or at Polaroid laughingly dismissed the possibility that digital cameras could eliminate their positions or their companies? How many leaders at Digital Equipment Corporation, the company that invented the mini-computer, had the same attitude when Ken Olsen, their founder and CEO famously stated in a 1977 talk to the World Future Society, "There is no reason for any individual to have a computer in his home?"

There is a phrase, "Necessity is the mother of invention." Its corollary is "Success is the mother of complacency."

Our parents and grandparents lived and worked in a world in which their entire careers could survive the pace of innovation. Today, companies and the leaders who manage them must operate on the assumption that theirs may not last through the year.

How does a leader survive and thrive in an environment which is governed by the possibility that it could all go away tomorrow? How do you manage your job and your career as if the job you do today will disappear any minute? How many leaders would feel ill prepared if and when they are called into a similar Monday morning meeting? Are you one of them?

Ask yourself, Am I prepared? Welcome to the "Me" Enterprise.

PART II
The "Me" Enterprise

"Digitization is here to stay . . . your job isn't!"

Chapter 5

The Emergence of the "Me" Enterprise

Emergence

Noun

1. The act or process of emerging.

2. Evolution. The appearance of new properties or species in the course of development or evolution.

3. A response to the phenomenon of "You are on your own!"

"Me" Enterprise

Noun

1. An individual who exhibits excellence in leadership in the digitized, corporate environment of the 21st century.

2. Someone who excels in a corporate environment by applying the attitudes, values, principles and behaviors of a self-employed entrepreneur.

3. An individual whose singular focus is creating, selling and delivering value to their employer or customer.

4. A corporate culture of excellence achieved through results-oriented entrepreneurship and individual accountability.

There's something happening here . . . What it is ain't exactly clear . . ."

—Buffalo Springfield

The technological revolution or "digitization" of the workplace has generated unprecedented innovation and opportunity for businesses. Yet that same revolution has also created new and equally unprecedented levels of competition, forcing businesses to innovate more, improve productivity and reduce costs. These demands for corporate survival translate to greater demands on workers, with sometimes only marginal consideration given to the impact such demands have on the workers, their jobs and their careers.

As demands in production, time-to-market, and lower pricing at higher quality have increased, so have the expectations for employees and leaders, as has their risk level for remaining employed. The dramatic pace at which businesses are consolidating, reorganizing, merging, acquiring, being acquired, or closing down has created a dramatic disruption to jobs and careers, a disruption largely viewed as little more than an unavoidable consequence of corporate survival. The workplace has been stood on its ear, as have many of the conventional views about employment, management, and leadership.

The traditional relationship between employees and their employers was once described in terms such as "fraternal, collegial and familial," terms that described a symbiotic coexistence in which one could not survive without the other. CEO's of past generations (predominantly men) acted as surrogate fathers, preaching a gospel of family and togetherness. In exchange for loyalty and hard work, the company was always there to look after their employees' best interest. CEO's preached messages such as "employees first" and "you will always have a home here." Beyond a salary and a career, companies provided their employees an emotional refuge of protection, comfort and well-being in a world that was viewed as cold, ruthless and highly competitive.

Technology and its many downstream repercussions have drastically altered that dynamic.

The fraternal relationship that companies and their employees once enjoyed has been reduced to one of survival. A relationship, once characterized by loyalty, support, and collaboration, now exists on those terms only as long as the employee can meaningfully contribute to the company's business challenges with greater speed, greater quality, and at a lower cost. Above and beyond skills, reliability, attitude and loyalty, careers are increasingly being governed by "what can you do for me today?"

Though some CEOs are attempting to revive that familial relationship with their employees, they are few and far between. The harsh realities of economics and competition have made them the outliers. In the main, companies have abandoned policies of "no lay-offs" and perennial raises and promotions, in exchange for phrases such as "in the best interests of our shareholders." What was once the message "You will always have a job here" became, although couched in much rosier "corporate speak" terms, "We must do what must be done to survive; and you are on your own."

Employees have been caught in the middle of this fight for corporate survival, many feeling unprepared, emotionally and financially abandoned, and left with the nagging question, "How do I survive now that I am truly on my own?

The "Me" Enterprise

Today's technology-driven climate has generated endless opportunities. It has yielded better products and services, faster cycle times, improved efficiencies and more precise performance and quality. But in doing so, it has made the challenges for businesses to keep pace even greater and employability for employees, managers and leaders even more difficult.

Corporations are riding an unprecedented wave of non-stop technological innovations which have redefined the economy, the nature and the pace of doing business, and the way employees are expected to perform. Yet, until now, there has been little guidance on how employees adjust to, survive and thrive in the digitized workplace.

Corporations are redefining the nature of their relationships with their workforce. More and more, corporations are moving towards contract labor, part-time employees, and other models designed to attract the best and the brightest, while retaining maximum flexibility for the company at lower costs. Many companies are subscribing to employment practices much like those of the National Football League with its players – short-term contracts with high incentives, but no long-term obligation.

Increasingly, employment agreements are being crafted to allow the company to get maximum production from its workers, while retaining an "out" clause that allows the company to part ways with minimal financial impact, should the company find the need to shift gears, shift directions and shift its workforce in order to remain competitive.

Yet, there are employees who are emerging to survive and thrive in this new environment. From entry level to "C" level, employees have cultivated a new mindset for how they manage their work life and their careers. They have come to view themselves less as an "employee," and more as a "self-employed entrepreneur" within the company in which they work. They are emerging to take control of their jobs and their careers.

They are the "Me" Enterprise!

The "Me" Enterprise is a new paradigm in employee behavior in terms of how employees engage and interact with their employer, and how they take responsibility for themselves and their careers in their work environment.

The "Me" Enterprise is a set of values, attributes, disciplines and behaviors in which employees apply the same basic operating principles to manage their careers, as does their company in managing their business.

The "Me" Enterprise is an employee, manager or leader who creates his or her own mission statement, own strategy and own blueprint for success.

The "Me" Enterprise is an enterprise of one. One who acts as his or her own CEO, VP of Marketing and VP of Product Development. One who develops and executes his or her own game plan for competing in and remaining relevant and employable in today's business environment.

The "Me" Enterprise is one who treats the company in which they work not as their employer, but as their customer.

The "Me" Enterprise is one that exhibits the behaviors and qualities of a perpetual, sole proprietary start-up.

The "Me" Enterprise is one who takes full advantage of the resources and benefits provided by their customer or employer, but recognizes and operates knowing ultimately that they must fend for themselves.

The "Me" Enterprise is a response to the perception that companies have left employees "on their own." It is the means by which employees are taking control of their own careers.

The "Me" Enterprise" is the consummate win/win proposition, to their employer, their customer, and their own careers. They are a major contributor to their employer's and customer's success, governed and driven by results. Yet they are also the most agile and least burdensome in adjusting to the constant changes that occur in their company and in the marketplace, thus making themselves the most marketable among other prospective employees.

How are successful leaders surviving and thriving in the world of digitization and "Uberization?" What are the attributes, attitudes, skills and behaviors that govern their approach to their work; their interaction with their employers, their customers and their peers; and their performance? Why are they succeeding where others are not?

When asked why some members of his leadership team seem to be able to rise above the day-to-day distractions of politics, competition and performance pressures more effectively than others, the CEO of a leading energy firm, said two words: "Confidence" and "Ownership!" When asked to elaborate, he said:

The good ones know their value. They know they are good because they focus on delivering what our customers want, and what I want. And they aren't distracted by outside noise. They know that if our company were to close down tomorrow, they could get another job, as good if not better than the one they have today.

Furthermore, they act as if this is their company. Though I am the CEO of this company, my best leaders all behave as if *they* are the CEO. They take responsibility, they make decisions, they solve problems as if this is their company and the company's ultimate success depends on them.

The "Me" Enterprise and the Millennial Factor

In assessing the styles, qualities and attributes of successful leaders in the digitized workplace, we began to see somewhat of a generational distinction between those referred to as "Baby Boomers," and the emerging workforce characterized as the "Me generation," or "Millennials."

The "Baby Boomer" generation remains the largest segment of active workers in the workplace and continues to occupy the largest percentage of corporate leadership roles. It was Boomers who launched the technological revolution in the 1990's. It was the drive, creativity and ingenious innovations of Bill Gates, Steve Jobs, Larry Ellison, Ken Olsen, Jeff Bezos and hundreds of other entrepreneurs that got the technology revolution underway. Their innovations were complimented by their strengths in organizational management, optimism, determination and their willingness to work long hours to see their ideas come to fruition in the marketplace. They grew up in organizations with large corporate hierarchies, and their leadership styles and strengths were shaped and molded by that environment.

Millennials, in contrast, have resisted the traditional top-down, corporate structure. Many, in fact, operate as if there is no hierarchical chain of command. They have no reservations about going directly to anyone in the organization if they have a question or a great idea, even the CEO. Rather than hierarchy, their chain of command is governed by curiosity, creativity and networking.

They are well educated, technology oriented, self-assured, able to multi-task, have plenty of energy and ideas, and do not hesitate to express those ideas. They have high expectations for themselves, and work diligently to achieve those expectations. However, they tend to pursue their work challenges differently, with more of a work/life balance than their predecessors.

Contrary to the conventional wisdom and concerns voiced about the "Me Generation" not having the drive or the relentless work ethic of their parents, Millennials have proven to be very aggressive and relentless in their work life, only with a different approach than their parents. Where Boomers had a tendency to save their vacation days, as if for a rainy day, Millennials tend to use their vacation allotment, and then buy more to enjoy their pursuits outside of work. They take sabbaticals; they take time off to hike the Appalachian Trail; they take extended maternity leaves; they take "gap" years. Millennials work just as hard as their parents, but with a far greater emphasis on equal time for their families and their personal interests.

Additionally, as author Leigh Buchanon writes in "Meet the Millennials," "Another defining characteristic of Millennials, beyond being creative and masters of technology, is that they are determined to do well by doing good. Almost 70 percent say that giving back and being civically engaged are their highest priorities."

Millennials have grown up at a time when information is available instantly. Through a Google or Wikipedia search, answers to even quite complicated questions can be found. As such, Millennials have emerged as a group that wants to work on new and challenging problems, with a strong belief that they are the ones skilled enough to find creative solutions.

The Millennial generation is the largest age group to enter

the workforce since the Baby Boom generation, and as this group continues to grow in size, they will soon emerge as the largest segment of corporate leaders.

In many respects, Millennials tend to personify the attitudes and behaviors that define the "Me" Enterprise, and their skills, characteristics and values also appear to represent qualities that will be successful in the era of digitization. They are agile. They work effectively in teams. They are fluent in technology, and bring a strong social mindset to their work.

Could it be?

Having embarked on our search for the qualities of the composite prototypical leader in the digitized workplace, here to now, predominantly led by Baby Boomers, is it possible that one very significant key to that search may lie in the characteristics, habits and skills of Millennial workers? Is it possible, if not a natural evolution, that as we entered the 21st century led by a generation of Baby Boomers who launched a corporate revolution, the next generation is emerging as the best examples on how to take that revolution to another level?

Could it be that, with one foot planted in the corporate traditions of the 1980s and '90s, and the other wading into the murky waters of the next wave of a technological revolution, the "Me" Enterprise is emerging as a rare combination of the best qualities of two generations of leaders?

Extracting the best from each generation, the blueprint for the "Me" Enterprise" is indeed a blend of the attitudes of the "Me" generation, combined with the wisdom and experience of their predecessors.

In the meantime, employers are increasingly challenged to find the right balance between a workforce that spans two generational styles. Can they sustain a corporate culture that retains its "Boomer" talent, and at the same time, attract and retain valuable Millennial employees, now and into the future?

Chapter 6

A Blueprint for the "Me" Enterprise

Blueprint

Noun

1. A process used chiefly in copying architectural and mechanical drawings, which serves as the basis for a master plan.

2. A print made by this process.

3. A detailed outline or plan of action, i.e.: a blueprint for success.

Blueprint for the 'Me' Enterprise

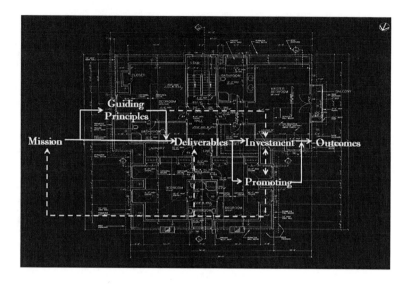

In recognition of the fact that there are attitudes, skills and characteristics that the past two generations of workers and leaders offer in surviving and thriving in the digitized workplace, we asked the essential question. . . . How do we, in practical and organized terms, extract the best of both worlds to form a structured prototype or blueprint that can be used as a foundation for others? What would a combination of attributes look like and how would they be constructed to create the optimum "Me" Enterprise leader?

What are the common attributes? And how do we define them? If we want to shape and mold leaders who can consistently survive and thrive in today's workplace, what do we teach them? In today's economic, political and market uncertainties, what are those qualities, characteristics and skills that enable the good ones to consistently deliver what the customer and the CEO want, and not get bogged down in distractions or trivialities? Can they be defined, quantified, replicated?

In the past ten years alone, hundreds of books, articles and management programs have analyzed, examined, dissected and catalogued these elusive qualities, habits, styles and personal traits that differentiate the successful leaders from less successful ones. They are numerous, and they vary on many points; but they all tend to converge on five key ingredients. These are the characteristics that consistently define effective leadership in this era of digitization, and we see them as the key ingredients of a Blueprint for the "Me" Enterprise.

1. **Mission** – They possess and are guided by a well-defined, personally relevant mission; a sense of purpose that defines who they are, what they are about, their passions and their aspirations as a leader;

2. **Guiding Principles** – Their behaviors and their decision-making are governed by a set of guiding principles that shape their personal and career values and behaviors, which include a style and set of interpersonal skills that promote working together as a team, problem solving, conflict resolution, and empowering others;

3. **Deliverables** – Their work is geared toward producing tangible, results-based deliverables that they consistently provide to their employer, their customer and themselves;

4. **Invest in Self-Development** – They invest in themselves. They take responsibility for their own personal and professional development. They are "lifetime learners," dedicated to continually re-learning and reinventing themselves and their craft.

5.   **Promoting** – They take assertive steps to ensure that the outputs and value of their work are visible, to their employer, their customer, and the marketplace, without appearing self-promoting or egocentric.

Knowing what we know today, if we were to attempt to mold and shape the ideal leader for the digitized economy of the 21st century, we believe its foundation would be built on these core ingredients. These are the ingredients that we propose will serve as the blueprint for the "Me" Enterprise.

The following chapter will examine each of these core ingredients, including examples and illustrations of their practical application, their value to employers, customers and peers, and why they are the foundation of leadership in the digitized economy.

Mission

Blueprint for the 'Me' Enterprise

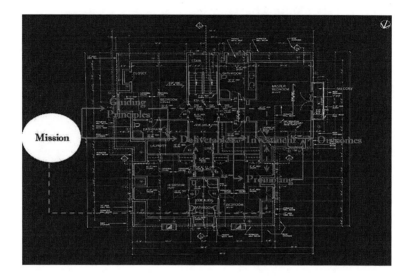

Mission statements are a staple of the corporate world, and they are emerging as a foundational element of the "Me" Enterprise. Corporate mission statements serve as a declaration about why the company exists, and they provide a constant reminder to the company's employees, shareholders, customers and partners about what the founders envisioned when the company was founded.

BrandVox, a company specializing in corporate branding, describes a mission statement as needing six elements to be effective:

- It should be short and easy to repeat;
- It should focus on a specific problem;

- It should use plain language;
- It should put a stake in the ground by avoiding words like "help"
- It should set a big goal; and,
- It should start with an action verb.

To illustrate their point, BrandVox offers a sampling of company mission statements that, in their view, "get it right." A few of these are listed below:

1. "We strive to be the global leader in the sporting goods industry with brands built on a passion for sports and a sporting lifestyle" – Adidas

2. "We seek to be the Earth's most customer-centric company for four primary customer sets: consumers, sellers, enterprises and content creators" – Amazon

3. "To inspire and connect with women to put their best selves forward every day." – Ann Taylor

4. "To connect people with their world, everywhere they live and work, and do it better than anyone else" – AT&T

5. "Turning moments into memories for our guests" – Fairmont Hotels

6. "To help customers improve and maintain their biggest asset – their home." – Lowes

7. "To give people the power to share and make the world more open and connected." – Facebook

8. "To organize the world's information and make it universally accessible and useful." – Google

As these examples illustrate, mission statements are intended to provide a sense of purpose, and in succinct fashion, answer these fundamental questions:

- "What is our purpose?"
- "What is our value to our customers?"
- "What is our pursuit of excellence that makes us stand out in the marketplace, and differentiates us from our competitors?"

Although mission statements tend to be modified and updated over time, they are typically written in a fashion that makes them timeless, with an ability to withstand changes in market conditions or the limited shelf life of a particular product or service.

The "Me" Enterprise Mission

Personal mission statements are fundamentally no different than corporate mission statements. In his 1989 best seller, *Seven Habits of Highly Successful People*, author Steven R. Covey put a personal spin on the concept of mission statements, as part of his second habit, where he says, "Begin with the end in mind."

The 7 Habits of Highly Effective People
Habit 2: "Begin with the end in mind"

Habit 2 is based on imagination—the ability to envision in your mind what you cannot at present see with your eyes. It is based on the principle that all things are created twice. There is mental (first) creation, and a physical (second) creation. The physical creation follows the mental, just as a building follows a blueprint. If you don't make a conscious effort to visualize who you are and what you want in life, then you empower other people and circumstances to shape you and your life by default. It's about connecting again with your own uniqueness and then defining the personal, moral, and ethical guidelines within which you can most happily express and fulfill yourself. Begin with the End in Mind means to begin each day, task, or project with a clear vision of your desired direction and destination, and then continue by flexing your proactive muscles to make things happen.

The "Me" Enterprise, behaving as a corporation of one, employs this principle. It effectively addresses those same fundamental questions and communicates its mission no differently than would a Fortune 500 corporation.

In helping his clients craft a mission statement, consultant Tim Berry outlines a series of questions that can be helpful in the creation of a mission statement for any "Me" Enterprise:

- Who is your company?
- What do you do? And why do you do it?
- What do you stand for?
- What markets are you serving? And what benefits do you offer them?
- Do you solve a particular problem for your customer/ employer?
- What kind of work environment do you want for yourself? Your employees?

There are a wide range of examples of personal mission statements, by both the famous and the not-so-famous.

Oprah Winfrey describes her mission as, "To be a teacher.

And to be known for inspiring my students to be more than they thought they could be."

Denise Morrison, CEO of Campbell Soup Company, employs a more comprehensive work-life balanced mission statement: "To serve as a leader, live a balanced life, and apply ethical principles to make a significant difference."

Anthony DiPietro, a New York based IT professional, describes his mission statement as, "To enlighten and serve my clients as to the value and the possibilities of technology, and to do so in a way that I am the first person they think of when they have a question about technology."

Amanda Steinberg of Dailyworth.com describes her mission as, "To use my gifts of intelligence, charisma, and serial optimism to cultivate self-worth and net-worth of women around the world."

Whatever your purpose, and whatever your goals and aspirations you have for yourself or your employer, your personal mission statement as your own "Me" Enterprise is your foundation.

Steve Cooper, contributor to Forbes Magazine, summarizes it beautifully when asked why you should write a personal mission statement:

> "When running a business things will get tough. If you don't know why you're doing it, things could become downright miserable during those times. A personal mission statement is your guiding light when things get dark. It might be easy to understand that your business mission is to create a suite of apps that will help educate children, but that doesn't answer the questions of why you are doing it. What is your personal mission statement? If someone were to type your name into their search engine, what would you want associated with it?"

The "Me" Enterprise Mission: "Promoting, Capabilities and Connections"

The mission of a leader who embodies the characteristics of the "Me" Enterprise is not dissimilar to those who employ the above mission statements. But when distilled down to its core elements, there are three essential ingredients that are at the heart of the "Me" Enterprise mission:

1. **Promoting** – A declaration and promotion of one's purpose, capability and personal brand to decision makers, to willfully undertake and solve complex problems and challenges;

2. **Capabilities** – A relentless pursuit to develop, strengthen and expand one's value through the development of capabilities; and,

3. **Connections** – An equal pursuit to establish and strengthen a personal and professional network of mentors, peers, executives and thought leaders.

Done correctly, with these three elements serving as the core of its mission, the "Me" Enterprise is transformed from a professional that attempts to push its way into a position of corporate strength and value, to one that is pulled into that position, by those mentors and thought leaders that become committed to its success.

Your personal and professional value and your personal brand are a bi- product of your mission; and your mission is the sum of the capabilities and connections you create and nurture, within your company, within your professional network, and within your community.

The formula below, in a vein similar to E=MC2, can be

considered a universal formula for the mission of the "Me" Enterprise:

$$M = PC2$$

Mission = Promoting x Capabilities x Connections

As an explanation, your mission, based on the development of your capabilities, is to actively and aggressively promote and position your capabilities to your network of peers, bosses, mentors and advisors.

With your mission clearly defined, the remaining elements of the "Me" Enterprise Blueprint speak to how that mission is fulfilled by guiding principles, values, strategy, governance, execution and other essential ingredients necessary to survive and thrive in the digitized workplace.

Guiding Principles and Values

Blueprint for the 'Me' Enterprise

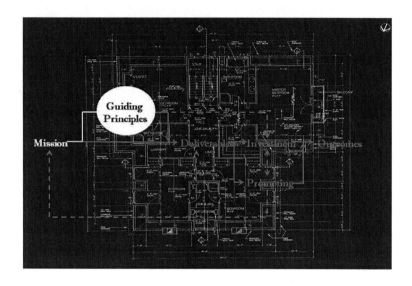

"Your beliefs become your thoughts,
Your thoughts become your words,
Your words become your actions,
Your actions become your habits,
Your habits become your values,
Your values become your destiny."

—Mahatma Gandhi

A mission serves to establish a sense of purpose . . . a sense of direction from which to move forward. As you embark upon that mission, the next question is what will be the rules that govern your journey? A defined set of guiding principles and values serve as the credo of the "Me" Enterprise leader, which have consistently proven to be a significant attribute that distinguishes them from the others. Your guiding principles are how colleagues, co-workers, employees, customers and bosses describe you when asked. They are the most defining characteristics in the creation of your personal brand.

These are the guiding principles and values that we have concluded best exemplify the "Me" Enterprise. We invite you to test yourself with each, in terms of your agreement, and in terms of your own behaviors and values.

1. You are self-reliant; you operate as if "On Your Own"

Though you may work in a corporation or company that is very supportive of you and your career, you do not confuse being "supportive" with being "responsible." Just as you are taught by the medical community that you must take charge of our own health care, you apply the same principle to your career. You actively seek out and embrace the support you are provided by your company, in terms of training, career guidance and opportunities, but you ultimately operate on the principle: "I am on my own. I create and execute my own personal plan, which enhances my value, in the eyes of my employer and my customer."

2. You employ the principle of "constructive dissatisfaction!"

Midway through their 2015 season, the New England Patriots football team won their eighth consecutive game and at the halfway point of their season, they remained undefeated, with eight more games to go. In the locker room, following their win, the Patriots players celebrated their success. That is until their coach, Bill Belichick, walked in and began to speak.

You are a good football team, and you are to be congratulated on today's win. But eight games is only half a season, with a very difficult second half of the season to go. Essentially, we have won nothing. Do not confuse today's win, or any of our previous wins this year, as success. Success can only be celebrated when we raise the championship trophy. Until then, we are a good football team, nothing more.

—Bill Belichick, Coach and GM
New England Patriots

Bill Belichick, for all of his accomplishments as a four-time Super Bowl champion, and all of his controversies as a football coach, embodies the definition of "constructive dissatisfaction." He would not allow himself or his team to be satisfied with past accomplishments. "Complacency," he said, "is the enemy of success." Of all the things Bill Belichick has been accused of throughout his career, complacency is not one of them. As the game changed, as the competition changed, and as the make-up of his team changed, he changed his strategy, tactics and in many cases, re-invented his team to achieve success amidst those changing conditions.

Similarly, when Christoph Franz, outgoing CEO of the German airline, Lufthansa, was asked what his greatest accomplishment was, he replied:

Creating a culture that values change within the company is probably what I'm most proud of. Lufthansa has always been a very inward-oriented culture, but competitive pressures require you to be flexible and open to new ideas. Always be self-critical and vigilant when we look around at what our competitors are doing, and ask, 'What can I learn from them?'

"Constructive dissatisfaction" acknowledges success and past performance, but does not rely or rest on the past. Nor should you be lulled into believing that past successes will ensure tomorrow's success.

The concept of constructive dissatisfaction recognizes and acts on the need to celebrate the success of your career, but to relentlessly find the weaknesses in your performance, and turn them into strengths, an essential ingredient to perpetual success!

3.You are committed to the highest level of business ethics:

"If it comes down to your ethics versus your job, choose ethics. You can always find another job."
—Sallie Krawcheck CEO and Co-Founder, Ellevest

The dedication to business ethics, we believe, represents the highest priority of values and guiding principles.

The adherence to ethics, as does the deviation from those ethics, begins with the smallest of acts . . . fudging on travel expenses . . . shortcuts on customer commitments . . . taking business time to conduct personal business . . . overlooking or giving a wink of the eye to employee transgressions . . . disregarding or overlooking established procedures or processes . . . transparency, or lack thereof, in employee communications.

These seemingly inconsequential actions have shown the potential to be the first steps onto a slippery slope that can result in an increasing pattern and a corporate culture which can lead to major consequences.

Beyond the seemingly minor and insignificant individual transgressions, there are more egregious examples at the corporate level which can further erode the quality of an organization and its individuals, and in some cases, destroy careers and corporations.

One example is the subtle, sometimes overlooked practice of tying individual financial incentives or bonuses for an executive to quarterly or annual profit and loss results. To a degree, this is the right thing to do; but in some cases, executives have exorbitant financial incentives, or punitive actions tied to their results. This is fertile ground for fostering bad or unethical behavior. Many veteran executives and corporate leaders know of examples where the quarterly or annual financial results of a corporation were adjusted or manipulated to maximize profits. Deferring expenses, inappropriately recognizing revenue and other such practices to exaggerate the financial performance of a company, and at the same time, enhance the financial benefits to its leaders, are just a few ways which not only illustrate an absence of business ethics, but have brought individuals and corporations to their knees.

Consider the recent corporate scandals of Toyota and Volkswagen, or the tattered history of CEO transgressions such as Kenneth Lay (Enron), Bernard Ebbers (WorldCom), or Dennis Kozlowski (Tyco).

Large or small, ethical violations are not only a violation of employee and shareholder trust, they are also a violation of what separates exceptional leaders from marginal or failed leaders. The slope is slippery, the line is fine, but the impact is real.

As a leader, you are not only responsible for your personal ethics, you are responsible for the ethics of your employees and your corporation. A dedication to ethics is a dedication to learning the governance laws and regulations of your company, teaching them to your employees, and inspecting their compliance.

You know that your ethics are integral to your brand. And

you know that what has taken years to create could be destroyed in one moment, one careless act. You are on the right side of this essential element of who you are, and of all who are responsible to you, as individuals and as professionals.

4. Perform or Perish! You deliver results, and are prepared to stand by those results.

> "Some of us will do our jobs well and some will not. But in the end, we will be judged by only one thing . . . the result!"
>
> —Vince Lombardi

Style is important. Knowledge is important. Cooperation and responsiveness are important. Efficiency is important. But if those qualities do not end in results, they are soon overlooked and forgotten. The overriding mantra of the "Me" Enterprise is a page out of the civil rights movement in the United States during the 1960's, "Keep your eyes on the prize!"

The "Me" Enterprise fully recognizes that he or she lives in a "perform or perish" world, and knows that their value, success and ultimately their employability will be driven by their ability to produce results! The adage, "It's a dog eat dog world" has never been more apropos. The demand for talent is high, and the competition is even higher.

Sole practitioners such as doctors, lawyers, contractors and consultants have always operated under the reality of "perform or perish." Their businesses do not survive if their patients don't get better, their clients don't win, or their customers don't get better results. With the ever-increasing pressures of competition and market demands, "perform or perish" is quickly emerging as the norm in the corporate world. More than ever, corporate stakeholders not only expect, but demand results, and not later, but now! If you're not feeling the squeeze in your workplace yet, hold on. It won't be long before you do.

The ramp-up period for a leader coming into a new company has traditionally lasted several weeks, if not months. There was a "honeymoon" period that provided a chance to get acclimated and into the flow of the new work environment. That honeymoon period today is weeks, if not days, if there is any at all. Performance expectations begin Day 1, with minimal hand holding or on-the-job training.

This is not to say that results are always achieved, or *should* always be achieved precisely according to plan. Things happen. Plans get derailed. Performance suffers. In those cases, however, when you know the results are not going to be achieved as planned, you take the responsibility to communicate the issues in advance, and take decisive actions to narrow the gap. When all is on track to achieve the results as planned, communicate frequently. When things are NOT on track and the expected results are in jeopardy, communicate even more frequently.

The corollary to "perform or perish" is "no surprises." The corollary to your brand is, simply, you make things happen!

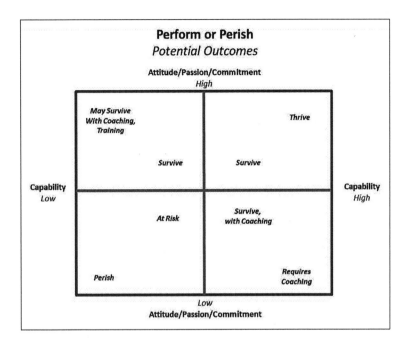

5. You embrace the concept of "I" with "We!"

"I with We" is the concept described as (1) the extent to which successful leaders target, commit to and embrace a goal or an objective; (2) how they motivate and inspire their team to embrace that same objective; and (3) how they take their commitment to a higher purpose beyond quantifiable results.

Having a higher ambition is one thing, but it's quite another to actually deliver on the promise of creating superior economic and social value quarter after quarter and year after year. This is the work of leaders.

Developing yourself as a higher ambition leader involves discovering your true purpose—what impact you want to have with your life—and using your work as one channel for realizing that purpose. It is more than making the quarterly numbers or achieving a business objective. Those are both important but higher ambition leadership is about the long haul. Is your leadership helping to make the world a better place now—and after you are gone? Are you using each day to build an enduring legacy of positive contributions in the lives of stakeholders?

Such leadership requires both passion for a long-term goal and the tenacity to pursue it over a lifetime."

—"Leadership" Center for
Higher Ambition Leadership

When is the last time you were truly inspired by a leader? When is the last time you said, "I would run through fire" . . . go into battle . . . run through a brick wall. . . ." or other euphemistic phrase expressing your commitment and loyalty and admiration for an individual?

Is that how General George Patton was described by the soldiers that served under him in World War II? Patton was called on by General Eisenhower, the Commander for the Allied Forces in Europe, at a very critical time for the allies in their march to Berlin. He was given a mission to break through very difficult enemy resistance.

He had two options to plan and execute his mission:

The first option was to go to his leadership team with the mission they had been given, but have a blank slate in terms of the strategy they should employ to execute the mission, and allow his team to collaborate with him on defining the strategy and the plan by which to accomplish their mission.

His second option was to go off on his own, and formulate his battle plan, and then bring that plan to his team for review and acceptance. He would put forth his plan for review, for refinement, and ultimately for his team's commitment as to how they proceed forward.

Patton chose the second scenario. He wanted input from his leadership team and he wanted them to embrace his plan as their own. But he felt it needed to be his plan! He felt that he would be abdicating his leadership role if he did not provide them with his thoughts, his strategy, and his views from which to build a final version of his plan. General Patton chose "I with We."

Did Steve Jobs employ the "I with We" principle at Apple? Did he forego his vision and allow his leadership team to formulate the vision for his company, for the sake of buy-in? Or did he put forth his vision first, from which to gain their inputs and ultimate buy-in? What about Nelson Mandela in his pursuit to transform the nation of South Africa? Or Golda Meir? Or the many other great leaders in business, culture and politics?

These leaders were not distinguished just because of their talent. They became distinguished leaders because of their levels of commitment, their levels of passion and determination . . . and their ability to put forth a vision (I), and then draw others to their cause (We).

"I with We" is about not letting the "I" get lost in the pursuit of "We." It is about being clear, bold and assertive in the declaration of your beliefs, your vision, and your determination, and then challenging, inviting, and encouraging others to join you on that adventure.

"I with We" is an attitude and commitment of personal accountability, personal ownership and personal results, in support of the corporation, the business unit, and the team. "Beyond what my leaders ask of me, beyond what my team asks of me, I will learn the strategy, I will understand the objectives;

and I will put my stake in the ground (I), and then embrace all those who join me ("We").

6. You exhibit the new "high performance" behaviors in the age of Digitization

Saying someone "performs at a high level" can sometimes be a vague concept, difficult to quantify or describe. In an effort to establish a more concrete foundation for what constitutes "high performance behavior," in today's work environment, we have identified sixteen behavioral characteristics that are viewed as essential benchmark behaviors of excellence in the digitized world.

These elements describe the attributes, behaviors and environment which we believe are exhibited by the "Me" Enterprise to consistently achieve results that exceed those of their peers.

The High Performance 'Me Enterprise'

- They foster and thrive in a self-managed culture
- They consistently achieve a work-life balance
- They foster a culture of giving
- They engage in "talent mapping"
- They seek "performance based" rewards
- They sustain a "commitment to employability"
- They are externally or customer focused
- They promote team performance
- They believe in the power of "yes"
- They obtain proper tools and training to excel
- They are "fanatics" for technology
- They create envy, not jealousy
- They maintain visibility of their results
- They are knowledgeable about best practices
- They demonstrate a bias for action
- They aspire to leave a "purpose-challenged" legacy

The brand of the "Me" Enterprise in the world of digitization is that of a new age, high performance leader. One who has embraced the realities of the new corporate world order, and who has adjusted to those realities.

7. You are loyal to talent, not people

In many corporations, certain employees enjoy "protected" status. They are the ones whose loyalty to their boss assures them of job security and top consideration for promotions and other opportunities. Though they are convinced they have earned their positions and the status they enjoy on their own merit, many of their co-workers believe otherwise. "Protected" employees are a fact of life in the corporate world. It is human nature.

But it is not part of the "Me" Enterprise. Though you are known for being fiercely loyal, your loyalty is not simply to individuals, but to the talent and expertise they bring to your team, your company and your customers.

Loyalty to an individual, purely for the sake of loyalty, is not only a disservice to you and your company, but to the employee. It weakens their preparedness and ability to survive the increasing competitive nature of the digitized world. Like you, what loyalties they enjoy should be based on their commitment to continuous learning and self-development, and the value they bring to their team and their company.

That is the nature of your true loyalties.

8. You sense, intercept and act: Your formula for ensuring your customer's success!

In conventional business terms, being a "problem solver" is essential, but no longer sufficient. Not if you are to stand out from the pack. Being a problem solver is akin to "meeting" expectations. Exceeding expectations is when you sense a problem as it is or before it occurs, and solve it before it becomes a problem.

Recently, one of the authors of this book was with a group dining at a well-known, upscale restaurant, and when I placed my order, I asked for a glass of wine to be delivered with my entrée. Our entrees were delivered in a timely fashion, but they arrived sans wine. When I asked our waiter about my wine, he apologized profusely and hurried off, presumably to retrieve the wine. But after ten minutes, still no wine. Granted, it was a busy time. The restaurant was full and the waiter that was serving our table had more to worry about than our party, but I was growing impatient and less empathetic.

Before I had a chance to flag down our waiter again, however, the restaurant manager approached our table. He explained that he was monitoring our order fulfillment via his customer engagement software, and recognized that I had not received my wine. He apologized for the delay and inconvenience, and delivered a bottle of wine to our table (I ordered a glass), compliments of the manager. With a timely and relatively inexpensive gesture, the restaurant manager turned what was looming to be a very unsatisfying dining experience into one that was both satisfying and memorable.

Had he not intervened when he did, I, like many people, would have eventually summoned the manager to express my dissatisfaction. Or had I once again flagged down my waiter to eventually get the wine I had ordered, no matter how good the food, no matter how enjoyable the conversation, the evening would have been regarded as an expensive, yet unsatisfying experience. Had the restaurant, as many companies do today, sent out a text or email the following day, asking for feedback on our dining experience, the feedback would not have been positive."

Three factors seemed to have turned a potentially negative experience into a positive one. First of all, the restaurant manager had technology that afforded him real-time information regarding the status of all orders and transactions. Second, he was focused enough on the importance of customer satisfaction to be monitoring those transactions. Third, he took immediate, just-in-time action to turn what was becoming a negative experience, into a positive and memorable one.

The manager's gesture of providing a complimentary bottle of wine, and the timeliness of his gesture converted me from a "grumbler" to a "promoter" of the establishment. He sensed and intercepted the situation before it became an issue.

I continue to frequent the restaurant, and also have the added enjoyment of a personalized exchange with the manager during each of my visits. Had it not been for his actions, I would not have returned to the restaurant, and in addition, I would have advised others not to do so either.

In a similar circumstance, the manager of a major hotel chain was chatting with guests in the hotel lobby when he noticed a man struggling to navigate the hotel's revolving door entrance with multiple pieces of luggage. The manager immediately retrieved a luggage cart, intercepted the man as he entered the lobby, loaded his luggage onto the cart, and summoned a bellman.

The man thanked the manager and said, "I was just about to ask for a luggage cart. You beat me to the punch. What service!"

The hotel manager replied, "Service is when you don't have to ask for it!"

The hotel manager, like the restaurant manager before him, sensed the situation, intercepted a potential problem, and acted to solve it before it occurred.

The concepts of addressing and correcting problems used to be an annual function, during performance review time, or during the budgeting and business planning cycle. In today's environment, that is too late. Even quarterly, monthly or weekly corrections are too late. We are now living in a just-in-time world, and even that concept is being challenged . . . from just-in-time, to "just-in-before-time."

In all of your activities with all of your stakeholders, customers, employees, bosses and partners, you employ a "just-in-before-time" method of intercepting problem situations before they occur. You sense, intercept and act. That is your brand . . . sensing what is happening, and proactively taking steps to intercept a potential failure before it happens.

9. You are able to create "permanency" in transient times

The pace of business has moved to the fast lane. Product lifecycles have been reduced from years to months to weeks. The lifecycle of an engagement, or a project, or working relationships and partnerships, which once lasted for months, now last for days. The average time a leader spends overseeing the performance of a single team has been reduced from two years plus, to less than a year. Five year plans are non-existent. One year plans last less than six months. Annual sales quotas are adjusted quarterly. In summary, what was once "permanent" and predictable, is now highly "transient."

Conventional timelines have been reduced to shreds, yet many companies continue to employ business practices and processes that adhere to those conventional timelines, such as employee performance appraisal systems and customer satisfaction surveys. Annual performance appraisal processes and regularly scheduled customer feedback mechanisms are fast becoming untimely, perfunctory and largely ineffective in the digitized workplace.

Paul Hebert, an expert in designing and implementing business improvement programs, envisions a new generation of "transient leadership" inspired by of all things, an X-Box game he watched his son play, called "Halo." Hebert describes leadership as situational at best, dictated by an environment that can change from circumstance to circumstance.

> I think that being a leader today is situational at best. The current environment dictates who the leader is. The leader a few minutes ago may not be the leader in the next few minutes. In the business world the time frames may be longer (but not much) but the concept is the same. Workers today expect and understand that leadership is transient and are not fazed by those kinds

of changes. Whereas some workers may have grown up in environments where leaders lasted decades, today workers must be able to quickly change leaders based on the environment presented.

Second – the ability to shift leaders is predicated on having information on skills.

As in Halo – knowing what the person brings to the table is critical in order for a worker to shift alliances. Communicating and documenting skills will be one of the foundational blocks that will allow a company to leverage transient leadership.

Third – ongoing discussions on what worked and what didn't – as soon as the "battle" is over – are critical.

This will mean more candid conversations held as soon after the event as possible. We no longer have the luxury of months of preparation to discuss last year's marketing plan – we need to talk now and react now. That is the world we live in.

Individual leaders will change more quickly in the future and as with Halo – there needs to be a common theme for the company. For Halo, it is to survive and kill as many of the other guys as possible. For the business it needs to be that simple as well . . . simple enough to allow multiple changes in leadership without jeopardizing the organization.

Leveraging both technology and logic, you provide an element of permanence in a very transient business environment. At a time when leaders transition from one position to another measured in months, not years, leaving unfinished debris in their wake, you ensure that, when you move from one position to another, your employees, your actions and any lingering issues are transitioned cleanly. Your brand is described as one who does not pass the buck to your successor, in what is a transient, "pass the buck" environment. You recognize the transient nature of today's corporate environment, and provide continuity and clarity from one engagement to the next, and from one leadership team to the next.

10. You never stop doing customer related work. Even as a leader, you remain a "Player/Coach"

As you returned from the Monday morning meeting in which you learned that your Division had been acquired by another company, one of the recurring thoughts in your head was the possibility of being removed from your leadership role and reassigned an individual contributor role. Though you enjoyed your status as a leader in your current role, and though the thoughts of a "demotion" were unsettling, you reflected on how much you enjoyed the "purity" of your life as an individual contributor, and how much you enjoyed solving customer problems every day. You thought that once you brushed up on your technical skills, you could actually enjoy getting back into the role as an individual contributor.

As your mind continued to wander through the maze of possible outcomes from this acquisition, you also thought to yourself that whether you remained in a leadership role, or were reassigned to an individual contributor role, you needed to stay current with your technical skills regardless of the outcome. You also needed to spend more time with customers in either role.

That was the one element of clarity you gained in the sudden confusion and uncertainty of this very uncertain situation . . . maintaining your technical skills and maintaining customer responsibilities should never end, regardless of your position.

In the world of consulting, the work breakdown of an entry

level consultant is typically 80% client-based work, and 20% administrative and training. The work breakdown of a senior Managing Principal is just the opposite . . . 20% client-based work, and 80% administrative. The lesson to be taken from the world of consulting is, no matter how senior your position, no matter what your primary responsibilities are, you ALWAYS retain some degree of customer or client-based responsibilities, regardless of title or level within the organization.

The practice of promoting technical specialists into leadership roles, and away from customer based responsibilities, leads to multiple unintended consequences:

- The employee is promoted from an area of expertise, to one of lesser expertise;

- The employee is, in many cases, placed in a position that is neither their natural work habitat nor their passion;

- The company loses an excellent content expert, as do the customers who were the recipients of that expertise; and,

- The employee's value in the marketplace diminishes as his or her domain expertise gradually fades and becomes out-of-date as they move further from their content knowledge into their role as an administrator.

In contrast to promoting from "content expert" to "administrator," the alternative practice is one that many companies are taking from consulting firms and other organizations. It is a practice in which they develop career paths for technical or content experts that allow them to grow within the organization. But they never transition into an administrative role that takes them completely away from their company and the customer who benefits from their expertise.

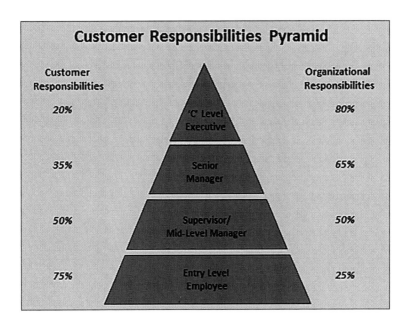

Many sales leaders, in addition to assigning all of their accounts to individual sales representatives, also assign certain accounts to themselves. They maintain their sales role, along with their sales management responsibilities.

Have you found yourself promoted out of your content or technical expertise? If so, a strong recommendation is to find your way back to your domain knowledge . . . either in your current role or a new one. Never lose your skill. Never lose your value. Hold dearly and continue to cultivate your expertise. It is an essential element of the "Me" Enterprise, and an essential element of your ability to survive and thrive in the digitized workplace.

Your brand must reflect one whose content knowledge remains current, and customer value remains high, regardless of your position in the organization.

11. You step up in times of crisis! You lead from the front . . .

It is said with admiration, "Firefighters go into a burning building when other people are trying to escape." The "Me" Enterprise does not seek out crises; but when crises arise, they step up. They do not shy away. There are endless examples of leaders who stepped up in the midst of a crisis, just as there are examples of those who shied away.

In 1982, an unknown person or persons replaced Tylenol Extra-Strength capsules with cyanide-laced capsules and deposited them on shelves in a number of pharmacies and food stores in the Chicago area. The poisonous capsules were purchased, causing the deaths of seven unsuspecting consumers. Johnson & Johnson, the parent company of McNeil Consumer Products Company which makes Tylenol, was suddenly put into a position of having to explain to the world why its trusted product was killing people.

Johnson & Johnson Chairman, James Burke, immediately stepped in to take a series of prompt actions, including taking the product off the shelves of pharmacies, and engaging in a highly visible and transparent media and communications blitz with the public throughout the crisis. His stated #1 priority was, "How do we protect the consumer?"

Scholars have come to recognize the leadership that Chairman James Burke showed in a time of crisis was instrumental in regaining consumer confidence in the Tylenol product, and as some concluded, saving the company itself.

On the opposite side of the spectrum, there is a more recent example of a leader shying away from a crisis, and suffering a very different fate. This occurred during the BP oil spill in the Gulf of Mexico in April of 2010. At the height of the crisis, then BP CEO Tony Hayward was being interviewed and stated,

"We're sorry for the massive disruption it's caused their lives. There's no one who wants this over more than I do. I'd like my life back!"

Hayward's comments baffled the press and the public as he clearly communicated that his number one priority was not the crisis and the impact it was having on the environment and the people who were affected by the spill, but the disruption to his own life. Soon after this interview, Mr. Hayward was relieved of his duties as CEO.

Chances are, as the CEO of your own "Me" Enterprise, you will not encounter crises as dramatic as the Tylenol scare of 1982 or the BP Oil spill of 2010. But you will encounter crises. And when you do encounter crises, resist the temptation to flee from the burning building. Step up and make yourself available. This is not to propose that you overstep your bounds and your authority, or take unnecessary risks. Instead, in times of difficulty and challenge for your customer, you must make yourself visible and available.

Are you recognized today, as part of your personal brand, as someone who leads from the front in times of crisis? Ensure that you are.

12. You realize that you are voted on and re-elected to your role every day!

Every interaction with customers, employees, colleagues, bosses and partners is constantly scrutinized. Unlike politicians who are elected and re-elected every two, four or six years, today's corporate leaders are assessed and voted on every day, with every engagement, with every interaction. This is a reality that continues to intensify as the world becomes increasingly virtual. Every email, phone conversation, video call, town hall meeting or text message provides constituents, bosses, colleagues and employees an opportunity to assess, judge and make determinations about your job performance, your career and your future.

In the conventional world where engagements, job assignments and positions were longer lasting, leaders were afforded time to let their constituents get to know them and learn their value as a leader. Those opportunities were based on face-to-face interactions, as well as phone discussions, emails and customer related activities. Over time, even if first impressions were less than favorable, leaders had the time and the opportunity to gain credibility.

Today, job assignments are shorter. Teams come together and disband more quickly. Interactions between team members and their leaders are based more on emails, conference calls and remote communication, rather than face-to-face interaction. In some cases, teams never even meet face-to-face. How does a leader establish and maintain their credibility in the digitized, virtual world? How does a leader recover from poor decisions, poor results, or in some cases, even poor performances in a meeting, a conference call or other forums?

Following an organizational shake-up at his technology services firm, Steven Landry was transferred from his operational role, based in the Midwest, to take over an underperforming sales team in Oklahoma and Texas. Steven knew his value as a leader. His firm knew his value as a leader. But the team in Texas and Oklahoma that he was about to lead had never heard of Steven Landry.

His first interaction with his new team was via conference call. Steven, as was his verbal style, was low key, monotone and mild mannered in his introduction and his responses to questions. After the call, one of the Texas sales reps looked across the table at his outgoing boss and said, "Does this guy even have a pulse?"

Steven eventually met his new team face-to-face, and

eventually developed a solid working relationship, but by his own admission, he said the team lost 2-3 months of solid sales productivity while they were assessing and feeling ambivalent about their new leader.

The "Me" Enterprise recognizes the importance of every interaction, every engagement and every circumstance in which stakeholders can assess, judge and vote. You must operate on the principle, "I am being assessed in my role every day, and all interactions, large and small, are part of that assessment."

Treat every day as if you are auditioning for your job, and treat every interaction with team members, customers, bosses and stakeholders as if you are making a first impression. You and your company will be the better for it.

13. You believe in and embrace diversity

One of the world's largest, multi-national technology giants recently brought together a worldwide team of leaders for an executive development program. The participants were organized into groups consisting of members from different geographies and different cultures to undergo a week-long series of problem-solving exercises.

During one of the evening exercises, the Conference Coordinator was summoned to meet with one of the teams that was experiencing a major conflict which resulted from a remark made by one of the participants. After meeting with the team, the Coordinator discovered that a team member from Australia proposed that the team's strategy for the evening exercise should be the "K.I.S.S." Principle, "Keep it simple, stupid!"

The team leader, who was from Japan and not aware of this phrase, which is fairly common and well known in western cultures, felt the remark was directed at him personally, and took offense to being called "stupid!"

The conflict required more than three hours to resolve. Given the combination of language and cultural differences, much explanation, discussion and many apologies were required to get the team back into the objectives of the exercise. But now, they were more than three hours behind the other teams they were competing against.

During the same executive development program, another team, the team that won the competitive exercise at the end of the program, reported a significant event that contributed to their team success. One of their team members was from Poland. He spoke English, but not fluently, and exhibited a somewhat shy personality. He seldom spoke during several of the initial exercises, and his teammates concluded after the first two days that he would have little to offer in the completion of their exercises.

On the evening of Day Three of the event, the team was focused on a drawing being constructed on the whiteboard at the front of the room. One of the team members noticed that their Polish team member already had the solution drawn out on a piece of paper, but had been reluctant to assert himself or his solution into the team discussion.

When asked to draw his solution on the whiteboard, the shy Eastern European team member reluctantly did so. His teammates immediately recognized the value of his solution, thus saving them significant time and catapulting the team to winning honors at the conclusion of the event.

Though you may not work for a multi-national firm, chances are very high that regardless of the size or nature of your workplace, you work in, with and amongst co-workers of other cultures, other countries and other languages.

In the 1960s – 1970s, diversity in the workplace was predominantly about race. In the 1970s - 1980s, it was about nationality. In the 1980s – 1990s, diversity in the workplace was about gender. You can now add age to that equation. With the convergence of the Boomer generation and Millennials, more and more workers are older than their bosses.

Diversity is about recognizing the value in our differences, be they cultural, racial, gender, nationality or age; and leveraging that value.

Diversity. . . . Be sensitive to it. . . . Recognize it. . . . Leverage it . . . Be known for it.

14. You believe in a work/life balance

In the increasingly competitive environment of our workplace, job security is paramount, sometimes resulting in the temptation to not take time off, not take vacations, and not engage in those activities with our family, colleagues or friends that recharge our batteries. Additionally, with emails, project plans and calendars fully available to us on our smart phones, tablets and PCs, it has become more and more difficult to escape our jobs at all.

Our work has become a 24/7 endeavor, and more and more companies and individuals are in search of creative ways to rediscover a work/life balance.

Slack Technologies, a cloud-based team communication business, was just named Inc. Magazine's 2015 Company of the Year, and is doing its part. The motto in Slack offices is, "Work hard and go home!"

The $2.8 billion start-up promises to make working "simpler, more pleasant and more productive." Less than two years after launching, Slack has more than 1.7 million users and $45 million in annual revenues. Just as interesting is that the company's CEO, Stewart Butterfield seems to support a growing understanding that working hard doesn't and shouldn't mean working endlessly. Inc. Magazine's profile of the company notes that the offices are pretty empty by 6:30 PM, a stark contrast to the norm for technology companies and especially for start-ups.

Earlier in his career, Butterfield used to put in 60-plus hour weeks and expected everyone else to do the same. But now Butterfield and his co-founders are all parents, and they have been dutiful in making Slack a place where grown-ups with lives outside the office feel welcomed and supported.

Facebook CEO Mark Zuckerberg recently announced that his company is instituting a four month leave program for employees, husbands and wives, who are new parents. Other companies are instituting similar policies to help their employees declare a firmer line between work and family.

More and more, companies and individuals are recognizing that a work/life balance is not only a healthier approach to personal and professional success, it is an essential one. You are one of them.

Despite the pressures of your work, you find ways to achieve that balance. You compartmentalize. You declare certain times as "off time" . . . times when the phone and emails are turned off. During family meals, during Little League games or soccer games, or at other times that should be devoted to your children or your family, you find ways to compartmentalize. When you are at work, you are at work, without distraction; when you are with your family, likewise, you are with family, without distraction. This applies to all other aspects of your life. You compartmentalize.

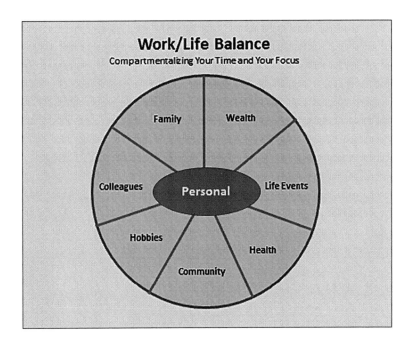

15. You believe in giving back

Robert Baden-Powell was a lieutenant-general in the British Army and is best known for founding the Boy Scouts. He is also credited with the quote:

"Leave it better than you found it." The essence of his teachings and his writings was the simple message, find ways to give back to your community.

Through guest lectures, volunteer work, civic organizations, teaching at the local community college or vocational school, your brand reflects the knowledge and value you can offer others in your company or community, and a willingness to share that knowledge with others.

You also recognize that the concept of giving back to your company or to your community is not as simple and straightforward as it sounds. You recognize that what you offer must have recognized value.

A senior executive of an American based multi-national firm took his first trip to Japan, to meet and visit with the company's Japanese executives. During his two week stay, he visited plants in Tokyo, Kyoto, Fukuoka and Nagano, and attended many dinners and social events in his honor along the way. Throughout his visit, he learned many Japanese social customs and business practices, which for him were both surprising and enlightening. He was enthusiastic about his new discoveries and was eager to share his learnings within his company. Upon his return, he organized a series of "lunch and learn" workshops for his staff, which he entitled, "The Essentials of Doing Business in Japan." He organized the luncheon sessions into five sections, to be delivered on five consecutive Wednesdays, and aggressively promoted the upcoming sessions through posters, leaflets, emails and conference calls.

On the first Wednesday, only two people attended, both of whom were back office workers who had no occasion to visit Japan on behalf of the company, but were "curious." The second Wednesday, neither of the two returned. Concluding that there was no interest, the executive cancelled the remaining sessions.

When he expressed his disappointment in the lack of interest in his workshops to a fellow executive, his colleague said, "Most, if not all of our staff who will conduct business in Japan, have already been to Japan, and are well aware of the local customs and business practices. They probably didn't see any real added value to the sessions."

You embrace the concept of giving back, but in doing so, you ensure that there is legitimate value in what you offer, with willing and eager recipients who will embrace your knowledge. That is the validation of your value as a teacher.

The concept of giving back to one's company or one's community has profound benefits, both for the recipient and the giver. When you teach, you learn. When you give, you get. When you celebrate others, you are celebrated. The laws of the Universe remain timeless and true . . . the more you give, the more you get.

DreamWorks co-founder, Jeffrey Katzenberg tells a story of one of his childhood heroes, Kirk Douglas.

I saw the movie Spartacus when I was just 10 years old. And from that day on, Kirk Douglas was a hero to me. Thirty years later, I found myself sitting next to him at a charity event. He had just addressed the crowd in a more eloquent, elegant, and passionate way than I had ever heard anyone speak before. I asked him where that passion came from. That is when he said, the most important words anyone has ever said to me: "You haven't learned how to live until you've learned how to give."

Giving back has always been viewed as being good for the soul. Research is now showing that it is also good for your health and your career. "Leave it better than you found it . . ." That principle is an essential element of the brand and the legacy of the "Me" Enterprise.

16. You recognize that both style and substance are essential to your success

The now famous televised Presidential debate between Senator John Kennedy and Vice President Richard Nixon was the turning point of the 1960 Presidential election. They were the first presidential debates ever, and the first to be televised, thus attracting enormous publicity and attention. While Nixon was still recovering from a hospital stay and refused makeup, looked pale and thin, Kennedy, who prepared for the debate at his family's Florida compound, appeared fit and tanned.

Following the debate, polls indicated that a strong majority of those who listened to the debate on radio believed Nixon was the winner. However, those who viewed the debate on television concluded Kennedy was the stronger candidate. After the debate, polls showed Kennedy moving from a slight deficit into a slight lead over Nixon, and eventually winning the presidency.

The overwhelming conclusion was that while Nixon may have possessed the substance, Kennedy's style, plus his substance, proved to be the winning combination.

Being the "smartest person in the room" can be helpful, but that is no longer sufficient for excelling in today's workplace. We are judged not only on how smart we are, or how much substance we bring to our jobs, but equally importantly, on how we bring it. Style matters. Be it stage presence in a meeting, voice presence on a conference call, or general demeanor in and around the office, how we present ourselves has become as important as what we present and how we present.

When a Phoenix based distribution company was preparing to do a television commercial, the CEO was asked to select one of his leaders to represent the company in the commercial. He knew exactly who he wanted for the spot. When asked about the individual by the account executive from the advertising firm that was filming the commercial, the CEO said, "He has the stage presence of a newscaster, and the content knowledge of a nerd. He's got it all!"

Does your brand reflect someone who "has it all?"

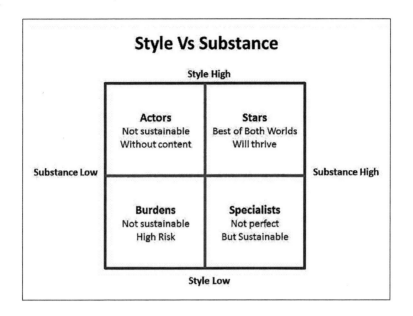

17. You have a highly trained "inner voice." You trust it, and you act on it.

Great leaders are many times characterized as having a "gut instinct" for things. In most cases, they don't know all the circumstances. They don't have all the facts. But in addition to the information they gather from others to help them make a decision, their most trusted advisor is their "inner voice," or their "gut!" They trust their inner voice, and sometimes, even when they have information contrary to their gut, they lean more towards their inner voice than to external information.

A 2011 study published in the journal of *Psychological Science* revealed that "all humans possess a 'gut feeling' or intuition. It is the exceptional individual that is more inclined to have the courage to act on them."

Gregory Vader was regarded as a rising star in a global Fortune 50 IT corporation. Over the course of his more than twenty years with the company, he held a number of sales management and general management roles, each with increasing levels of responsibility. But as his career advanced, he became increasingly disenchanted with his company, not with his performance or his responsibilities, but with the corporate politics and interactions that became increasingly internally concentrated. These gyrations, seemingly done to gain individual influence and favor, played an increasing role in management decision making.

With a reputation and a track record for being entrepreneurial, results oriented and largely apolitical, his inner voice had begun to speak louder and louder. The game he was now playing was governed by a different set of rules than he had been accustomed to. He concluded he was not having as much fun nor was as he as enthused for his work as he had been in previous years, and knew he needed a more entrepreneurial, less internally focused work environment. He decided it was time to look elsewhere.

After a careful reflection on his personal and professional mission and values, he organized and embarked on a campaign to market himself outside the company. He projected himself as an "entrepreneurial, results oriented, market savvy sales leader in a technology environment." Within a period of three months, Greg was presented and accepted a position as President to start up the U.S. subsidiary of an African-based technology company. He knew in his heart that sticking to his values, he would flourish in this new environment, as would those around him.

You have a finely tuned gut instinct or inner voice that you have come to trust. If your inner voice speaks, you listen, and more times than not, you act!

18. You engage in constructive confrontations to achieve results

In the annals of management and leadership study, scholars have drawn a distinction between two different types of power. One is "organizational or positional power," power that is derived from a leader having a direct line of authority over employees, and is thus able to exert their will by virtue of organizational rewards and punishments. The other is "influence or social power," power derived by one's leadership and interpersonal skills and ability to persuade.

In contrast to the traditional large organizations where leaders had ample resources with the direct authority to control those resources, leaders today have fewer direct resources under their direct control, thereby requiring them to rely on their influence skills to secure resources and direct those resources. As company power structures shrank and became more broadly distributed, thus creating a greater demand for "influencing" skills, books and leadership courses proliferated.

In their book, *Crucial Conversations*, authors Kerry Patterson, Joseph Grenny, Ron McMillan and Al Switzler, describe crucial conversations as those that occur "when the stakes are high, emotions run strong, and opinions vary, designed to yield major professional improvements in areas like productivity, quality, safety, diversity, performance and change management."

In their 1981 best-seller, *Getting to Yes: Negotiating Agreement Without Giving In,* authors Roger Fisher and William L. Ury described a method focused on the psychology of negotiation they called "principled negotiation," in which acceptable solutions are found by determining which needs are fixed, or absolutes, and which are flexible for negotiators.

Both best-sellers offer a variety of practical and methodical approaches and solutions to getting what you need in order to succeed in your company environment. We believe, given the accelerated level of competition, combined with the diminished level of time and resources, these principles need to be taken to another level . . . the level of confrontation.

As the pace of innovation increases, projects become more technical and more complex, with fewer resources having the required expertise. Your success is increasingly contingent on greater demands with fewer resources, both in terms of investment dollars and in terms of talent. In this increasingly competitive environment, the concepts of assertiveness and negotiations are necessary, but at times, not sufficient to achieve corporate objectives. When circumstances dictate, you are prepared to take your needs beyond being assertive, to the point of demanding results.

The same is true for your career.

In the climate of the "Me" Enterprise, you know the results you deliver; you know your value; and you know what you deserve in exchange for delivering that value . . . to your employer and your customer. You should not short-change yourself in getting what you deserve.

Whether it be to obtain resources or investments that are essential to succeeding on a project, gaining employee commitments, taking corrective actions, or getting a promotion, know your value, and demand what you deserve in exchange for that value.

One additional item to consider, as you engage in "constructive confrontations to achieve your desired results" is the issue of corporate politics. As long as corporations remain a human endeavor, there will be corporate politics. It is a universal reality you have most likely encountered, and will continue to encounter, and politics will always play a role in your need to assert what you require to be successful. Recognize it, acknowledge it, and constructively confront it. But do not be frustrated by it, and do not allow it to deter you from achieving the results you deserve in support of your brand.

Your brand is not one of being arrogant or obstinate, but it is one of demanding what you deserve from your employer or customer, just as you demand the same of yourself. In contrast to the fear of being perceived as "pushy" or arrogant, you realize that this level of assertiveness establishes respect. You are fluent in effective and timely confrontations. You stand up as a leader . . . for your team, your company, and for yourself.

19. You seek opportunities that employ the principle: Autonomy with Accountability

As the work environment has become faster paced, more technical, more competitive and more entrepreneurial, you too are more entrepreneurial. You have developed a style and an expectation in your work that your success is dependent on a work setting that fosters that sense of entrepreneurship . . . a work setting that holds you accountable for results, but with the freedom and the autonomy to make it happen the way you believe it should.

The concept of "autonomy with accountability" is one in which leaders are given a challenge; given the resources to successfully take on that challenge, allowed to undertake the challenge; and then held accountable for the results. You seek opportunities for you and your teams that offer just such an environment. You realize that a company, or a division, or a boss that does not afford you this type of entrepreneurial environment is a bad match for you. Since it is not suitable to your skills or your style, you will ultimately fail in such an environment.

The concept of "autonomy with accountability" is a major factor in your decision making criteria when you consider what jobs you take, what bosses you want to work for, what Divisions you want to work in, and what companies you want to work for.

As a result, you experience three distinct benefits:

1. You continue to refine your skills by virtue of the challenges you undertake and the problems you solve;

2. You continue to be customer focused, also fostering and enhancing your brand and skills;

3. Your talents become increasingly visible in the marketplace, thus furthering your marketability.

20. Your Communication Style is central to your Personal Brand

There is an expression that says, "Your language speaks volumes." That expression is not about the language of your nationality; it is about what you say and how you say it to others . . . and the interest you show in what others have to say.

There are many characteristics that define the communications style of effective leaders, but three are most significant:

*   They ask questions more and they give directions less – This is perceived by some to be a contradiction in effective leadership, as "leaders" are supposed

to give directions, not seek it. However, asking questions is one of the most powerful and underused tools that leaders have in their toolbox. Asking questions is the primary means of gaining insight. It is also a powerful tool in establishing credibility and solidifying relationships.

- They listen more than they speak – This, too, may seem somewhat paradoxical to the concept of leadership to some, because "leaders" are supposed to have a lot to say. To the contrary, listening is the companion piece to asking questions, and if you don't listen to the answers, the questions are meaningless. "Leaders" cultivate "followers" by virtue of the genuine interest they show in others. And interest in others is best conveyed in the form of listening to what others have to say.

- They demonstrate the "Art of Nuance." They recognize that the world is not black and white. They appreciate the "grey" in company matters and business matters. Their responses are not bombastic or absolute. They are measured and thoughtful in what they say, and how they say it, and they resist the temptation to be the person who has THE absolute right answer.

Find the most effective leader you know . . . someone you trust, respect and would follow . . . and observe them in action. Chances are very high that you will see them demonstrating these three, seemingly insignificant, but powerful communications techniques.

In contrast to conventional expectations of leaders, your communications style is one of "talk less . . . tell less . . . ask more questions . . . listen more . . . and be reserved and nuanced in your declarations."

"Listen, learn," and to paraphrase the words of President Theodore Roosevelt, "Walk softly and embrace the grey."

21. Connections, Connections, Connections – You Build and Nurture Your Network

You realize that one of the cornerstones of your mission and your brand is your ability to create and nurture connections. You develop deep and sustained relationships within your organization, including with bosses, peers, colleagues and employees. You extend those relationships out into the marketplace, to include customers, partners and competitors.

You offer guidance and insights to your connections, just as they provide guidance and insights to you. You find and create opportunities for your connections, just as they find and create opportunities for you.

You recognize that connections are the mother's milk of your career, and nurture them as one of your most valuable assets

22. You cross the "Digital Divide" to digitize your own "Me" Enterprise"

As the world around you has embraced technologies and moved to the concept of digitization, so have you. As the companies you work for, and the customers that you serve embrace technology to improve operational efficiencies, reduce costs and expand their market reach, so do you.

Charlie Harris has enjoyed a comfortable and successful career in the food processing industry. He began his career working in a processing plant unloading fruits and vegetables from trucks onto pallets, and progressed to become the Vice President for Plant Management for a major food processing plant in Georgia, when he requested a two week leave to attend a training program called, "Welcome to the World of Technology." Harris enjoyed his work, but felt he was behind the times in terms of new technologies and new practices that were overtaking his industry.

"I felt like I was on the wrong side of the digital divide. I came into this business when everything was done manually, and now, all I see are automated machines doing what people used to do, and I felt like I didn't know the business anymore. I want to work for another 10-15 years, and if I'm going to survive, I've got to learn this business all over again."

Charlie Harris is one of many who have been caught up on the "wrong side of the digital divide," and recognized what he had to do to survive.

You too, realize what you have to do to survive. You have migrated from your rolodex to electronics and social media to expand and build your network of contacts. You have moved from requiring an administrator or secretary to create your documents, to creating your own. Working from your "Mission" formula, M = PC2 (Mission = Promoting + Capabilities + Connections), you actively use blogs and other forms of social media to promote your brand, expanding your audience from hundreds, to tens of thousands.

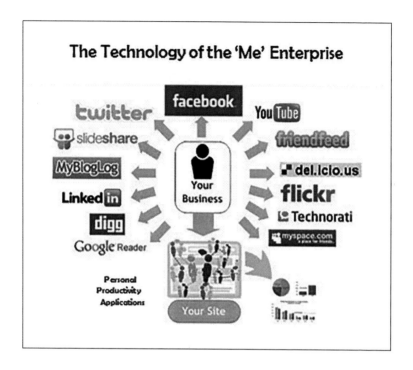

You embody the principles and practices of digitization, technology and social media in how you execute your day-to-day activities, and in how you develop, promote and enhance your personal brand. In turn, your brand reflects one of being highly productive, self-reliant and well connected.

23. As you are succeeding in your current assignment, you simultaneously prepare for your next assignment

Actors, freelance writers, consultants and other variations of self-employed professionals are always working two agendas: The first is their current assignment. The second is getting their next assignment. What is your next assignment? And what steps are you taking to position yourself for that next assignment?

Your next assignment may be within your current company, with another company, a partner, or even a competitor. It may be within your current career field, or it may be a transition to another career path. Whatever your current role, and whatever next step you are contemplating, your continued professional growth and success is dependent on you continuously working these two agendas: Your current assignment, and your next assignment.

* * *

Your values and guiding principles are a reflection of who you are. They are your brand. Your values project your beliefs, and in turn, your beliefs shape your behaviors. As a result, more than anything else you say or do, you are defined by your values. It is our belief, from our own experiences, and the many discussions we have had with successful leaders, this collection of values and guiding principles best exemplify the underpinnings of successful leadership in today's corporate workplace. They embody the substance and the spirit of the "Me" Enterprise.

Deliverables

Blueprint for the 'Me' Enterprise

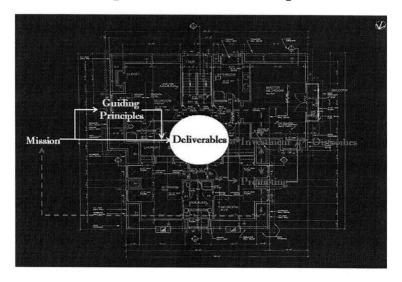

Leaders are ultimately judged on accomplishments, on what they deliver to their customer, their employer, their stakeholders. The same is true for prospective employers, who ultimately ask in the vetting process, "What have you delivered? What have you accomplished?"

"Deliverables" are the results a leader produces for his or her employer or client. They can be measured in terms of products created, sales or revenue achieved, profits realized, processes improved, or a project completed in accordance with specifications, time and budget, or some other end result. They are typically concrete, quantifiable and unambiguous.

Deliverables are essential to any personal or corporate success, and can vary from job to job, and from individual to individual. That, in our examination of deliverables is not what caught our attention. What *did* catch our attention was the emergence of a pattern or a framework in which deliverables are consistently achieved by successful leaders.

What qualities are consistently embedded in what, how and why successful leaders deliver in regard to the expectations and commitments to their employer and their customers? We found four distinct elements:

1. **Strategy** – Their deliverables are framed in the context of a defined winning strategy or game plan

2. **Governance** – Their deliverables are executed in accordance with the proper governance, ethics and oversight of the business.

3. **Technology** – They effectively and liberally employ and leverage technology as a differentiator,

   and,

4. **Execution** – They effectively and efficiently execute in accordance with their defined plan, and are able to quickly adjust to their plan when confronted with unforeseen circumstances.

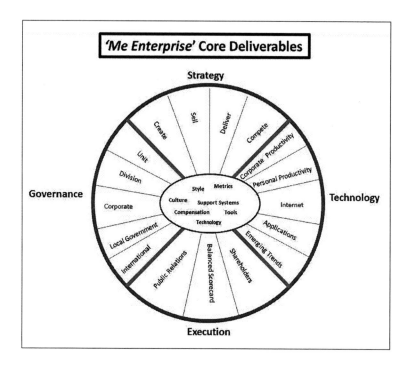

These elements, and their respective sub-elements, serve as the four pillars that govern the formulation and execution of deliverables of the "Me" Enterprise leader. And while all leaders, be they "C" Level executives, mid-level managers, or first level supervisors, have responsibilities in each of these elements, their emphasis and the degree of responsibility in each is typically determined by their level of leadership.

"C" Level Deliverables

As a "C" Level executive, while you have ultimate responsibilities in each of the four elements, your primary day-to-day activities and accountabilities are in the areas of (1) creating, communicating and driving the over-arching strategy for the business; and (2) defining, communicating and ensuring that the business is executed in accordance with governing policies, laws and regulations. Given the emerging role of technology in the workplace, as a "C" level executive, you may also find yourself increasingly involved in the technology aspect of the business, both as it relates to technology strategies, and to how those technologies are employed in delivering products and services to your customers.

Finally, though you seldom deliver the results as a "C" Level executive, you are always accountable for the results. As President Harry S. Truman so poignantly stated when asked who was responsible for policy in his administration, "The buck stops here!"

Mid-Level Managers

Mid-Level Managers serve as a bridge between the executives who formulate strategies, and the troops who execute and comply with those strategies. As a mid-level manager, you serve as your company's linchpin, ensuring that executive level strategy, governance and technology are properly translated, communicated and implemented by project teams and individual contributors, and that those teams have the resources to achieve their objectives, i.e., processes, materials, technology and training.

You have the additional responsibility of providing oversight in the execution of corporate deliverables; and communicating feedback to the executive ranks regarding conditions on the ground . . . what is working, what is not working and recommendations for changes, adjustments and improvements.

The hierarchy in the US Military, as in most military organizations, consists of three levels:

- **Commissioned Officers** – Generals, Colonels, Majors, Captains, Lieutenants, etc.

- **Non-Commissioned Officers (NCOs)** – Master Sergeants, Technical Sergeants, Staff Sergeants, Sergeants, etc.

and,

- **Enlisted Personnel** – Corporals, Lance Corporals, Privates, etc.

In her book entitled, *Backbone: History, Traditions, and Leadership Lessons of Marine Corps NCOs*, author Julia Dye outlines how Non-Commissioned Officers (NCOs), characterized by their judgement, enthusiasm, determination, bearing and unselfishness, serve as the backbone of the Marine Corps in terms of how they receive military strategy and objectives from their commanders, and effectively transmit those objectives to the various units under their command, and ensure that their units are properly equipped and prepared to execute those objectives.

Mid-level managers are the NCOs of the corporate world . . .

First Level Supervisors

First Level Supervisors also serve as NCO's in their company, but at a unit or team level. They are accountable for the execution of the plan and for providing feedback to their leadership teams as to status, progress, what is working, what is not, and recommendations for improved execution.

As a first level supervisor, you are typically the member of the leadership team that is closest to what is going on within the organization and with customers. As such, you are the first to know whether policies and strategies are working or not working; if those policies and strategies should be changed or adjusted; and you are responsible for recommendations about how they should be changed or adjusted.

As a first level supervisor, you occupy a critical role in (1) ensuring proper execution of the corporate strategy, and (2) serving as the trigger for making changes and improvements in what is now working and what could work better.

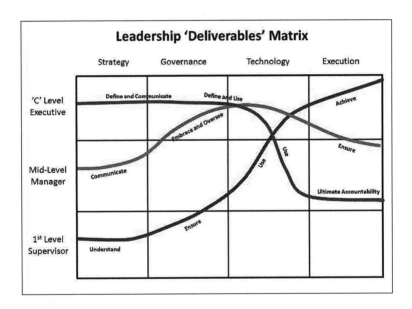

Some guidelines to consider, as you execute your deliverables. . . .

There are a number of factors and trends, which we have outlined in other sections of this book, that are becoming dominant components of the digitized marketplace. Some of these factors, in our view, must be essential considerations as you contemplate your deliverables. Consider these our recommended guidelines for you to incorporate into your thought process as you define and execute your deliverables.

Be a "Stractician" – As the rate and the pace of change continues to intensify, the timeline and the distance between strategy, tactics and execution continues to shrink. Defining strategy and tactics are no longer separate and distinct activities. Think of yourself not as a "strategist" or a "tactician," but a "stractician," one who works in a continuous iterative fashion to define the strategy, execute tactics, and rapidly make adjustments as circumstances dictate.

Make Liberal Use of Technology – Rapid changes in technology, an undercurrent of this book, have become the overarching ingredient of every corporate enterprise. As such, technology should be as much a part of your company's day-to-day operations as are policies and procedures. Technology is pervasive throughout your company, and will continue to be even more so. Technology should be a foundational element in every department and every division's day-to-day processes. It should be inherent in all corporate policies and practices. And technology proficiency should be a major criteria in hiring and promotion practices, as much as the performance history and experience of each applicant.

Be an "IP Fanatic" – There is a fine line between you and your competition. Market differentiation is more and more difficult to define; revenues are harder to come by, and margins are growing thinner. An often overlooked area for revenue and margin improvement is in the area of intellectual property, or IP. Become fanatical in your examination of your products, your services, and your processes as potential sources of intellectual property, potential sources for new revenues and margins, and differentiation in the marketplace.

Be an "Uber Watchdog" – Just because your company, your division or your job have not yet been "Uberized," that doesn't mean they won't be. Do not be lulled into complacency. Intensify your radar and constantly be on the lookout for the increasing presence of disruptions to your business. New technologies, emerging competition and changing market conditions are happening at a frighteningly rapid pace. Fine tune your sensing capabilities to become an "Uber Watchdog," and have your contingency plans in place.

Beware of the False "Yes" – As Ronald Reagan said at the height of the Cold War, "Trust but verify." You, too, must take a trust but verify approach as your leaders and your teams execute their deliverables. Just as there are increasing pressures to deliver, so are there increasing pressures to say, "Yes, we can do that!" Your inclination is to answer affirmatively even when sometimes when they cannot deliver. Ask detailed questions; monitor closely; inspect often; and live by the mantra, "expect what you inspect."

Re-Engineer in Good times – You know the conventional proverb, "Don't fix it if it's not broken." You also know that when it is broken, you have no choice but to fix it. We propose a contrarian view to this conventional wisdom.

In bad times, you make changes, re-engineer and reconfigure out of necessity. You have no choice when things are not working. History has proven that, more times than not, re-engineering in times of stress and duress has achieved the exact opposite of the desired result. Financial and time pressures to make changes in times of hardship invariably lead to poor planning and even poorer execution.

Re-engineer not when times are bad, but when times are good. You have a higher likelihood of getting the financial investments required, and with a greater luxury of time and circumstances to get it right.

Re-engineer in good times to prevent bad times

Use Guerilla Tactics – Historically, when contemplating change, corporations formed committees, explored alternative practices or products or services, committees made recommendations, and executives made decisions to implement. Taking a page from military parlance, there are conventional tactics, and there are guerilla tactics. The current rate and pace of changes in the marketplace no longer afford companies the luxury of conventional, corporate wide approaches to implementing change. Guerilla tactics are more and more commonplace, and more and more essential. When contemplating change, instead of pursuing large, corporate wide make-overs, look for small units that can serve as laboratories or test beds to test and validate new concepts or changes. Execute and perfect in small pockets, then expand to the next, then the next, and then the next. The makeover will spread more rapidly, and will continue to be improved and refined as it spreads.

Maintain a "Zero Tolerance" in Governance – Nothing can bring a company down faster than a violation of government or corporate rules and regulations. A blind eye or a wink and a nod overlooking a minor policy infraction is the starting point of a culture of tolerance. Zero tolerance must be the norm. Not just at the executive level, but at all levels. Operational and financial audits and compliance reviews should be common fixtures in day-to-day operations. Everyone should be trained and certified in zero tolerance policies regarding corporate governance, and everyone should become corporate watchdogs to help detect and extinguish any violations of those policies.

Establish and Maintain an External Focus" – Companies have "customer facing" employees, and "internal support" employees. Do not let these distinctions influence how and where you place your focus. If your current responsibilities are customer focused, cultivate and grow your knowledge about your customer, your customer's customer, your competition and the marketplace in general. The more you know the environment and the landscape in which your skills are applied, the more effectively you will use those skills.

If your current responsibilities are more inwardly focused, do not allow that internal domain to be the extent of your knowledge domain. You, too, must understand your customer base, your competition, the marketplace that your company serves. Find ways to make direct contributions to your customers. Even if you are a financial analyst with no direct customer responsibilities, you have financial expertise that could contribute in some direct or subtle way to the value your company offers its customers.

As a leader, ensure that you and your employees are outwardly and not inwardly focused. Ensure that your employees are fluent in external market and competitive conditions, as well as the value and financial performance you realize with your customer base. Establish a culture in which all employees are focused externally, on the customer and on the marketplace.

Develop Customized Hiring and Promotion Practices – Employee and leadership transitions are happening at an unprecedented rate. 2-3 month or longer hiring processes create significant gaps in financial performance and morale. Develop rapid response hiring and promotion practices. Develop succession plans that support "just in time" talent development. Further, develop progressive compensation plans that entice and incent entrepreneurship, innovation and increased development and advancement within the company, including individualized compensation plans for the top 15%.

Numbers, numbers, numbers – In today's digitized environment, everything is quantifiable . . . customer data, financial performance, human resources and processes. From revenues, to costs, to profits, to operational metrics, to utilization, to customer satisfaction and beyond, you know that your performance is ultimately based on how you perform against those numbers. You also know autonomy and freedom from scrutiny comes when you perform favorably against those numbers.

Reaffirm, in every policy and guideline, every speech, every employee rally, and every corporate communication, the mantra "Results, results, results," and "Numbers, numbers, numbers."

Know your numbers . . . ensure that your teams know your numbers . . . and deliver accordingly.

*   *   *

You, just like your company, are ultimately measured each quarter and at the end of each year on your deliverables. That is not new.

What is new is what you deliver and how well you deliver, and this is determined by how you deliver . . .

..... Within the context of a defined strategy;

..... In accordance with proper governance;

..... With liberal use of technology; and,

..... Executing with zeal, and the agility to adjust as needed.

Investment

Blueprint for the 'Me' Enterprise

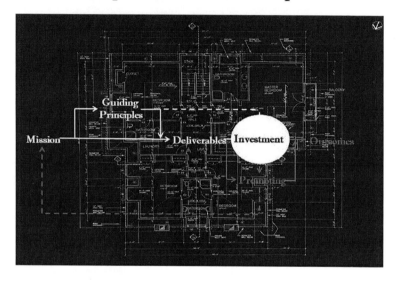

Corporations invest extensively, typically 8-10% of their annual revenues, in research and development to sustain their competitive advantage . . . as does the "Me" Enterprise. Like the company you work for, you should be investing in your own improvements. That investment comes in the form of training and development.

The concept of perpetual learning in the "Me" Enterprise is akin to the concept of "tithing" in a religious context, in which a dedicated portion of effort and investment is essential to the perpetuation of the enterprise

From formal training programs, to internships, to on-the-job apprenticeships and mentorships, training and development is viewed as the lifeblood of a corporation.

That is equally true for the "Me" Enterprise. "Investment," in the context of your career success, is defined as the investment you make in yourself, as in your commitment to your lifelong training and development. There is a term emerging in corporate circles that encapsulates this concept called, "Personal Knowledge Infrastructure."

At the risk of introducing yet another set of acronyms to the corporate lexicon, this segment examines and frames your commitment and your investment in your Personal Knowledge Infrastructure (or PKI) through a variety of learning practices and concepts.

To do so, we will use a concept with which you are already familiar, IQ or intelligence quotient, as a point of reference to encompass other dimensions that are essential to your commitment to lifelong learning.

GQ – General Knowledge Quotient – How proficient are you in the general practices, trends and technologies of the professional domain in which you work, i.e., retail, manufacturing, medicine, technology, telecommunications, government, etc. What is your knowledge level within your domain? What is your General Knowledge quotient?

EQ – Emotional Quotient – As the book "Emotional Intelligence" asks, what is your ability to recognize your own and other people's emotions or feelings, and use emotional information to guide your thinking and behavior? How effective are your interpersonal skills?

DQ – Digital Quotient – How proficient are you in the day-to-day technologies used by your company? And what is your knowledge level or fluency in emerging technologies, such as cloud computing, mobility, cyber security, big data and other macro-technologies?

CQ – Creative Quotient – What is your proficiency in creative problem solving, or the ability to create new solutions to undefined problems?

PQ – Political Quotient – What is your awareness level of the personal and professional interests and objectives of key players in your work group, division or organization? And to what extent are you in tune with their motives, interests, alliances and intended objectives?

Given the increasing levels and sheer pace of change in corporations today, perpetual learning is no longer a casual ingredient to success . . . it is an absolute necessity.

The centerpiece of a commitment to lifelong learning is the premise that the individual, not the corporation, is responsible for their own professional growth and development. As children, our parents engaged us in a wide range of learning experiences outside of our formal schooling. We took music lessons, karate lessons, language lessons, SAT preparation, in addition to a wide range of sports related activities, all designed to broaden our education and development. We fully leveraged the formal education experience in our schools, but we were not totally dependent on our schools for the totality of our development. Yet, when we complete our formal schooling and enter the world of work, there is a tendency to look to our employer as our sole source for training and development. This is not the recipe for success in the world of the "Me" Enterprise.

This section will put forth a framework for lifelong learning, or a "Personal Knowledge Infrastructure" by examining the core areas of learning inherent in the "Me" Enterprise, and also the various forms or types of learning experiences in which those core areas can be developed.

There are four core subject matter areas of the lifelong learner. . . .

1. **Learning your Specialty or Domain** – This area of training and development addresses the core subject matter of "how to do your job," covering the core skills and processes essential to your role and responsibilities within the corporation. The leader of a financial services firm takes training in the area of finance, auditing, etc., as does a sales leader in selling skills, product knowledge, etc., and the software engineer in design techniques and processes. "Domain" based training is essential in a corporation's efforts to prepare their employees to perform their various roles. It is essential, but not sufficient.

2. **Technology** – Other than the software and technology training necessary to perform certain day-to-day tasks, many corporations may view technology training as a secondary priority. In the eyes of the "Me" Enterprise, however, technology related training may be **the** most essential area of learning for long-term career growth and success.

   The digitized work environment continues to become and more technical, and the skills and expertise required to survive and thrive in that environment with each is changing daily, and the need to remain constant with those changes has never been more essential.

3. **Style** – A third essential element of lifelong learning relates to what many refer to as "style" elements. Those include topics such as interpersonal skills,

presentation skills, media training and other "soft" skills that are essential to success. While more and more companies are beginning to see the need for and are beginning to offer this type of training, the "Me" Enterprise does not rely on their employer to provide these essential skills.

4. **Investment in Yourself** – This element of personal investment is an investment in your life outside of work; your lifestyle. From personal finances to carpentry to electrical repair to hobbies, such as boating or survival skills, a complete investment in your development includes that which goes beyond your livelihood, to your life.

The second dimension of the lifelong learning framework is how, or by what means, lifelong learning occurs? Learning typically occurs via four methods:

1. **Formal education or training** – Structured training programs that are conducted in a traditional classroom, or via some form of distance learning medium such as webinars and video conferences.

2. **Relationship based Learning** – Creating informal, yet structured learning experiences through mentors, coaches, networks or other group sharing experiences;

3. **Experience Based** – Informal, yet structured learning experiences gained through customer engagements, "post-mortems," de-briefs, or other means of self-assessment;

4. **Teaching** – Learning by teaching others, a concept sometimes referred to as L.U.T.I. (Learn, Understand, Teach, Inspect)

Outcomes: Personal Knowledge Infrastructure

	Formal Training (Classroom/Online)	Relationship Based Learning (Mentors/Peers)	Experienced Based Learning (On-the-job/Internships)	Learning by Teaching (L.U.T.I.) (Teaching/Coaching)
Domain Knowledge (Job Content)	*Foundation for New Capabilities*	*Validation, Guidance, Wisdom*	*Strengthen Domain Capabilities*	*Inspire Your Organization*
Technology/ Software (Technical)	*Staying Current With Technology*	*Learning new Trends, Gaining Others Insights*	*Improve Productivity and Competitiveness*	*Improving Productivity Of the Organization*
Interpersonal/ 'Soft' Skills (Style)	*Formal Skills, Norms of Behavior*	*Gain Feedback, Validation*	*Strengthen, Polish Style*	*Model Style and Brand of the Organization*
Personal Life Training (Personal)	*Personal Life Goals*	*New Horizons Through Networking*	*Enrich Life Events*	*Promote Work/Life Balance in Your Organization*

With this framework as a guide, what are the essential characteristics or attitudes that drive your pursuits as a lifelong learner? To what extent do you adhere to the following guiding principles as you invest in yourself as your own "Me" Enterprise? We believe these principles should include the following:

1. You take personal responsibility for your own professional growth and development (personal and corporate).

While as the "Me" Enterprise, you aggressively leverage the full range of learning experiences offered by your employer, you also recognize that the ultimate responsibility for your development lies with yourself. The full range of formal training programs may vary widely from company to company, but all provide some form of training, both job specific and general development topics. Your ability to survive and thrive in today's work environment is dependent on you being a voracious learner, and taking active and aggressive advantage of those programs, whether specific to your current position, laying the foundation for a future position, or gaining general workplace or technical knowledge.

After completing her first graduate degree in India at the age of twenty-one, Pepsi CEO, Indra Nooyi, came to the U.S. to attend Yale's School of Management. Growing up in Madras, India, Nooyi described herself to her employees as a lifelong learner, and strongly urged them to be the same. Part of her message to her employees regarding their professional development, is:

1. Be forever curious. Examine every aspect of how your corporation works, and continuously ask "why" we do things the way we do.

2. Do not rely solely on your company for your professional development. Take advantage of all the training your company has to offer, but do not assume that your company is responsible for your professional development. You are!

2. You aggressively seek any and all training related to software and technology.

The pursuit of training opportunities is even more aggressive in the area of software and technology-related programs. In a world more and more dominated by technology, and more specifically, software technology, it is your challenge and your responsibility to remain knowledgeable about the technologies that drive your business on a day-to-day basis. Technology is no longer the domain of the CIO. It is an ingrained element of the DNA of the corporation, and should be the same for you.

There is a tendency in many circumstances to have assistants, administrators or colleagues take care of the technical side of our business routines and processes, while we concentrate on the customer or on the bottom line. We can argue that while that may be more productive and more convenient, history teaches us, it is not the wisest course.

Your value, not only to your business, but to your career, is shaped by your depth and range of skills and versatility. And a large part of that versatility lies in those day-to-day technology processes. How fluent are you in the personal productivity tools your company uses for its day-to-day business processes? Do you use them yourself? Or do you rely on an administrator for those activities? Do you know and use your corporation's management applications?

Tomorrow's product and services will have increasing software and technical content, including cloud computing, and cybersecurity and mobility. Tomorrow's leader must be proficient in those technologies. To what extent are you in tune with major technology trends, such as mobility, the cloud, big data, cyber security etc.? As the corporations become digitized, this commitment to technology will pay rich dividends.

3. You actively engage a network of mentors to leverage and learn from their experiences (Relationship based learning).

In support of your role as a perpetual student, your learning is governed in large part by the depth and breadth of your mentors. Mentors are community leaders, former bosses or colleagues or knowledgeable friends or acquaintances. They know what's going on in the marketplace, and they know you. Cultivate your network of mentors, and reach out to them often. Treat them as your own private advisory board.

Throughout your career, you will require advice. Learn to

seek it regularly and aggressively. Your advisory members can help you with knowledge and experience and can serve as a vital lead to your next career move.

Additionally, in recognition of the "Millennial" phenomenon and their natural affinity for technology, you have Millennials included in your board of advisors.

4. You learn from your successes and your failures (Experience based learning).

There is an expression that failure is our greatest teacher. That statement is partially true. Our successes are also a great teacher, and in many cases, an even more effective teacher. Our successes provide us the models of how we should be performing, the greatest blueprint for how to replicate them. Experience-based learning comes from our on-the-job experiences, and equally importantly, the feedback and reviews we receive from those experiences.

In lieu of traditional annual performance appraisals, many companies now employ "engagement based" feedback, which (1) is more timely feedback, and (2) more relevant to learning and career growth. If your company employs engagement based feedback, ensure that you are taking away from those feedback sessions the good, the bad and the training and education to be pursued as a result of that experience. What are the career growth actions?

If your company does not employ formal engagement-based reviews, make your own. Ask your project team members, your colleagues, your bosses, and even your customers to provide structured feedback and suggestions for future learning recommendations. Engagement based reviews, formal or informal, are an excellent source of capturing and documenting your learnings from your experiences.

In addition, think about keeping a journal or a log to capture your own feedback and suggestions. Handheld technologies and recording apps make this practice easier and more effective than ever in collecting and documenting real-time feedback and learning actions. Many learning professionals view experience based learning as the most valuable in shaping and enhancing a career. Are you taking advantage of this invaluable source of learning?

5. You practice the concept of L.U.T.I. (Teaching)

A few years ago, a concept called "L.U.T.I." was introduced into the marketplace which offers a solid foundation for continuous learning through teaching:

Learn – Utilize – Teach – Inspect

The concept of LUTI is a means of ensuring that you are constantly learning the newest advances in your market.

Knowledge is the key to your survival and your relevance in the marketplace. And today's knowledge may not be tomorrow's knowledge. Technological changes occur every day, and competitive forces are changing every day. Your ability to learn and teach, are integral to your success.

No matter how you prefer to learn, be it reading, classrooms, seminars, online webinars, or other means, a portion of your time and effort should be devoted to learning new ideas, new concepts, new technologies and new practices, and teaching them to others.

In addition to learning from training programs in your company, to what extent do you volunteer to share your knowledge and experience by serving as an instructor in those programs? Do you teach classes at a local community college or at the local vocational technical school? Do you mentor others, either formally or informally? Or serve as a mentor or trainer in on-the-job training assignments?

The value of your learning lies in your ability to teach others as does the value of your role as a professional. Learn . . . utilize . . . teach . . . and inspect.

6. You take calculated risks to enhance your capabilities and your career.

It is human nature to find your niche, your comfort zone, and to reside there as much as possible. Those who truly thrive in today's environment, are willing to find the means and the opportunities to purposely go outside of their comfort zone. They are willing to take risks, stretch their muscles, develop new knowledge and experiences. Special assignments, international positions, leadership positions with big responsibilities but no direct reports, are all examples of taking calculated risks and developing leadership power.

Eric Schmidt had just become the CEO of a start-up that would be called Google, and was interviewing a high profile executive for a leadership role in the company. After reviewing the profile of the job and the ideal candidate, the prospective employee said, "I don't fit any of the criteria for this job."

Schmidt replied:

"You should take a risk and get on this rocket ship. When companies grow quickly and have a lot of impact, careers take off. When companies aren't growing quickly or their missions don't matter as much, that's when stagnation and politics come in. If you're offered a seat on a rocket ship, don't ask what seat. Just get on."

Investment guru and Chairman of the investment firm, Berkshire Hathaway, Warren Buffett summarized the concept, saying,

> "I've gathered the most wisdom from those who have taken risks and rocketed up the corporate ladder and helped others climb with them. Here, some valuable lessons on how to lead well, achieve more, and have fun doing it."

Like the corporation that invests a percentage of its revenues in the training and development of its workforce, the investment you make in your own "Personal Knowledge Infrastructure" is essential to your career growth and your success. Assess your PKI quotient, and make it your business, make it a part of your brand to become a lifelong learner.

My 'Pesonal Knowledge Infrastructure' Quotient

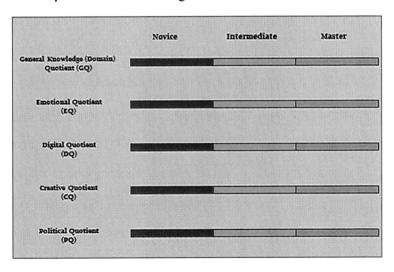

Promoting

Blueprint for the 'Me' Enterprise

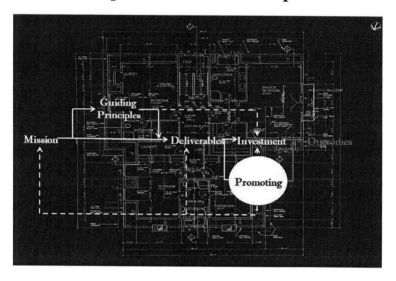

Whereas "Investment," as discussed in the previous chapter, is about developing your skills and expertise, "Promoting" is your ability to ensure that your expertise is recognized and sought after by others. The previous chapter on "Investment" poses the question, "To what extent do I effectively develop my knowledge and expertise?" In return, "Promoting" poses the question, "To what extent is my knowledge and expertise recognized and sought after?"

Promoting is the art of creating and inducing loyalty to you and your value, by your company, your bosses, your customers and your professional network. Promoting is the corporate equivalent of sales, marketing and brand development. It is about how you, as an individual, create, promote and sustain your personal brand. Just as corporations devote a significant percentage of their revenues to sales, marketing and brand development, so must you.

As individuals, there are many principles we can learn and employ from corporations about how they market and brand themselves in the marketplace. Corporations devote endless time, effort and expense to establish a corporate brand with the objective of creating "pull" in the marketplace. Rather than companies being in the position of having to pursue customers, the objective of corporate marketers is to effectively position themselves in the marketplace in which customers are pursuing the company.

To what extent does Lexus or Mercedes push its customers to buy its products? Or, by virtue of its marketing and brand development actions, do customers pursue their products? In addition to providing a quality product (Investment), what marketing and branding techniques or actions do those companies employ that enables them to be in a position of being the pursued, rather than the pursuer?

Similarly, to what extent is your personal brand such that employers and customers are pursuing you? Or, are you pursuing them? And what techniques can you employ to achieve a position in your marketplace similar to that of Lexus, Mercedes or other quality brands?

This chapter will examine five activities that can aid your efforts to effectively establish, sustain and enhance your personal brand in the marketplace.

They are:

1. **Assess** - Analyze your skills and passions, and determine how and where those skills and passions can best position you in the marketplace.

2. **Define** - Determine and publicize your personal and professional brand.

3. **Invest** - Invest in yourself to fulfill your personal brand.

4. **Promote**- Effectively position or market yourself to your prospective employers and customers in your marketplace.

5. **Repeat** - Continue the process of re-assessing and re-promoting as conditions change. (And they are always changing!)

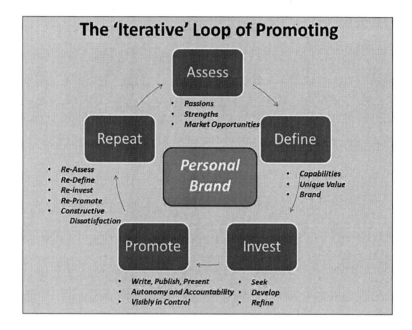

Assess

An assessment of your positioning in the marketplace boils down to finding the optimal intersection between (1) your passions, (2) your strengths, and (3) the market.

To "assess" is to explore, to analyze, to examine, and hopefully to draw some conclusions. In this context, to "assess" is to examine and try to answer three fundamental questions. And if you have alignment in your answers to these three questions, you have a significant head start in effectively positioning yourself in the marketplace.

1. What are my passions?
2. What skills and capabilities do I have in support of my passions? and
3. Is there a market for the things I love to do, and can do effectively?

You have an intimate knowledge of your passions . . .

There are many ways you can assess and determine your passions, including professional psychometric analysis that can provide a detailed psychological profile of your passions and interests. But if you are having difficulty drawing conclusions about things like passions and interests, and don't want to go the psychological route, we suggest you take a more colloquial route. Go to the local breakfast joint where retirees gather every morning to have breakfast and offer their commentary on world events, and ask them.

We did. We asked how they would define passion, and these are a small sampling of the answers we received:

"A passion is something you would get up at 4:00 o'clock in the morning to do, not because you had to, but because you wanted to.

"A passion brings joy! Even when it's challenging or difficult."

"Even when its hard work, a passion doesn't tire you, it energizes you."

What activities in your life fit the above criteria? The answers are a clue to the possibilities of aligning your work life with the things you love. It is also the first clue to finding your market niche.

Your strengths and marketable skills align with your passions . . .

The second question in your assessment is, "What marketable skills and capabilities do you possess in support of your passions?"

Neil Sampson grew up the son of a college music professor. With guidance and encouragement from his father, he began his musical training early, taking piano lessons at the age of three, and by the age of six, he was performing classical musical compositions in recitals and concerts throughout the area. He knew early in life that music was his passion.

As he grew, he pursued every opportunity he could find to perform . . . from classical piano recitals to jazz ensembles, to playing in rock and roll and rhythm and blues bands. Upon graduation from college, he started a family, and like many of us, he was confronted with the dilemma of doing what he loved, versus doing what would give his family the financial stability and lifestyle he wanted for them. He loved nothing more than playing music, but he knew the challenges that pursuing a career as a musician would create for his young family.

In graduate school, he had the opportunity to sit in the control booth of a recording studio while a symphony orchestra recorded a series of classical compositions. As the session progressed, he found himself becoming less focused on the orchestra, and more focused on the recording engineer and producer in the control booth. From that brief experience, he also found a way to merge his passion for music, with what would become his livelihood.

Today, Neil is a senior producer in a major recording studio. When asked to describe how his career as a recording engineer and producer came to be when he was such an outstanding musician, he replied, "I discovered, as long as it involved music, it didn't matter which side of the glass I was on."

Neil Sampson found his connection between his marketable skills and his passion. And hopefully, if you have not already, you will too.

Are there market opportunities that allow you to make a living and thrive doing the things you love?

In the 1980s, Bob Eskew had just completed his graduate degree in the area of Public Administration, and found work as a Program Manager for the US Department of Health and Human Services. His job was to plan, design and implement major initiatives for state welfare organizations. This gave him the opportunity to travel around the country and visit with state and local welfare organizations. He enjoyed his work, but he was less enthused and less optimistic about the state of his career trajectory, given the political environment and the negative connotations associated with welfare programs and the public sector.

On an occasion during a visit to a local welfare office in Boston, MA, he was given the opportunity to observe a work program that the local office had implemented in concert with a Boston based high tech company. During his visit, he met with the program coordinator for the high tech company, and struck up a conversation regarding their various roles. As the two learned more about their respective responsibilities, the high tech coordinator told Bob that, other than their clientele and their program objectives, their roles were virtually identical. He further shared that, given the explosive growth the high tech industry was undergoing, there was a growing need for Program Managers. He agreed to sponsor Bob's application, which ultimately resulted in Bob Eskew doing something he enjoyed, using the skills, training and experiences he had developed in the public sector, but in a brand new and emerging industry.

Bob Eskew found an opportunity to apply the skills and expertise he had learned as a program manager, but in a new and emerging market. Is your current market segment on the rise? Or is it ebbing? In what other market segments would your skills and experiences have value?

How do your strengths align with the market?

In his 1991 international best-seller, *Crossing the Chasm*, author Geoffrey Moore created a model in which corporations could assess how and where their products or services were positioned in the marketplace. Were their products or services in the early start-up phase of the marketplace, and positioned for a breakout? Were they enjoying mainstream success, but perhaps with their best days behind them? Or were they on the other end of the spectrum, nearing the end of life of their market appeal?

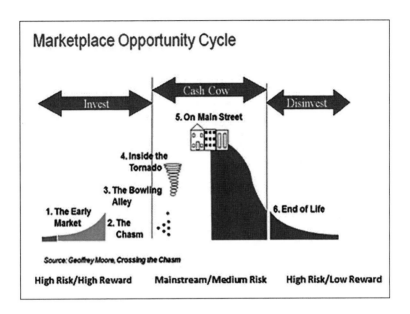

The Marketplace Opportunity Cycle, as crafted in Geoffrey Moore's bestseller is a model that can be used to assess your own personal marketability and how your strengths align to market conditions.

Geoffrey Moore's original model described businesses or products as being either in the "Early Market/Invest" phase; or the "Main Street/Cash Cow" phase; or the "Disinvest/End of Life" phase". Think of your own career and professional situation in similar terms:

Is your current job or career situation one that is in its early stages of market potential? Are you in an emerging market with new and exciting potential for growth? One with high risk, but the potential for high reward?

Or . . . are you in a more mainstream market? One that does not have the risk of a start-up or an emerging business, but yet does not have the same shelf life or growth potential?

Or . . . are you and your company, your profession or job situation one that has matured, peaked, and possibly seen better days? Is your current situation one nearing the end of its life?

The answers to these questions in your assessment are helpful in determining both the nature and the urgency of potential change in your current situation.

Within your company? Outside your company? Or on your own?

As you draw conclusions from your assessment of your current situation and future aspirations, how you would best define your future prospects, and where do those future prospects reside? Does your future best reside within your current company? Or, are your prospects stronger outside your current company, perhaps with a customer or competitor in the same market? Or even in a different market? Or, are your best prospects beyond the realm of being a traditional employee, and would you be better served as a contractor? An entrepreneur starting your own business?

Whether you use Geoffrey Moore's "Crossing the Chasm" model or another means to assess your position in the marketplace, the fundamental question is, "Where is my strongest potential for growth in the marketplace? In my current company? Outside my current company? As an entrepreneur?

Ask yourself the following questions: Are my skills and capabilities suitable for sustained career growth? What actions do I need to take to ensure I am well positioned for career growth? How do I best position myself in that marketplace? How will I define myself in that marketplace?

Define

A corporation's "brand" is how it is known in the marketplace. Their brand is how companies are perceived in terms of their products and services, and equally importantly, their value in the marketplace. Corporate brands are shaped by their name, the quality of their products and services, their messaging, and most importantly, their reputations.

What do you think of when you hear or see the term "Lexus"? Chances are, your reaction is, it's not just a car but one of the highest quality luxury automobiles on the market. Corporations spend a considerable amount of time, money and effort to ensure that their brand is a positive depiction of how they wish to be perceived in the marketplace, and Lexus currently enjoys a strong position in the automobile market. As market conditions change, however, corporations are quick to modify their branding accordingly.

In the 1990's, one of Lexus' automotive competitors, Audi, encountered a series of performance issues as well as a public relations nightmare when many of its vehicles would, without warning, suddenly accelerate, causing several accidents and deaths. Market analysts felt the problems were severe and damaging enough to drive the automaker out of business. In response, in addition to fixing the engineering problems that were causing the accelerations, Audi spent just as much, money, time and effort in repairing its brand.

Once the company was assured the problems were fixed, it launched an aggressive advertising and marketing campaign, with the tagline, "Excellence in engineering." The company not only survived, but remains one of the leading high-end, luxury automakers today.

In a cruel twist of irony, Audi's parent company, Volkswagen, is undergoing a similar crisis of confidence with its brand today, not related to its engineering, but to deceptive management practices. It will be interesting to see if the parent company is able to survive and thrive as Audi was able to in the 1990's.

Sometimes, under the more extreme circumstances, companies go so far as to change their brand altogether.

In 1996, low cost airline "ValueJet" suffered a crash in the Florida Everglades that killed 120 people. Following a massive series of legal and economic challenges, and a change in its management team and operating practices, the air carrier reintroduced itself to the marketplace as "AirTran." AirTran still operates today, and was recently acquired by Southwest Airlines.

Under far less dramatic circumstances, "Domino's Pizza" changed their brand to simply "Dominos," so as not to be viewed in the marketplace as offering only pizzas, but other food products as well.

The concept of corporate branding has now become an essential component of how individuals market and promote themselves. Oprah Winfrey, the former talk-show host and founder of the OWN network, addressed the 2012 class of Atlanta's Spelman College in her trademark no-nonsense way. Quoting from *The Color Purple* and referencing Taco Bell, Winfrey, a woman whose name itself is an instantly recognizable brand, stressed the importance of service and integrity over fame when building your own brand. Her advice:

> Let excellence be your brand . . . When you are excellent, you become unforgettable. Doing the right thing, even when nobody knows you're doing the right thing, will always bring the right thing to you.

In many respects you defined your brand, in the segment, "Values and Guiding Principles" in Chapter 6. What were those principles that defined you? What is your brand? How are you known to your employer? Your colleagues? Your competitors? Your customers?

If you ever want to know the answer to those questions, ask them . . . especially those who you trust to give you honest answers. Ask them to describe you and your performance. If you like what you hear, build on it and enhance it. If you don't like what you hear, be prepared to change it.

Reverting back to another old axiom, "If you don't know where you're going, how will you know when you get there?" Rule #1 in defining your brand is to know what you want; know what you would like to be doing; and know where you want to be doing it. While knowing these things is not always easy, keep one thing in mind – all of us have an inner voice inside of us telling us what we want to do with our careers, and our lives. The challenge is not letting that voice be drowned out by life's circumstances, and the need to simply pay your bills.

If you are overcome by that challenge, try this . . . In your quiet time, in your own way, put aside the inner and outer noise of why you cannot do something because you either have to pay the bills or deal with some other life obstacles, and let that aspiration that has resided inside of you for years find its way to the forefront of your thoughts. And when it does, seize it, and begin the process of defining yourself accordingly.

Your personal brand, be it by design or by happenstance, is how your company, your customers and your boss answer the following question . . .

"The best way I would describe_is_"

There is an expression that says, "If you don't define yourself, others will." When they do, what will their description be? As you begin the thought process of how you define your personal brand, we suggest that two phrases that must be included . . .

". . . impeccable value . . .",

and

". . . technological prowess . . ."

Regardless of your profession, or your job proficiency in your profession, or how you position yourself in your particular market segment, it is our belief that those two elements must be an inherent component of your brand if you are to survive and thrive in today's market.

"Impeccable value" is all encompassing, from how you perform your work, to how you treat your employees and your customers, and to how you deliver quality results.

"Technological prowess" must be an essential element of your brand simply because, whatever you do, in whatever capacity or whatever career field, technology is and will continue to be a growing element of your work.

However you choose to be known, and however you choose to promote yourself in the marketplace, ensure that those two elements are included.

Invest

Just as you "invest" in your skills and expertise development, you also invest in the marketing or promoting of your expertise.

Traditionally, corporations devote 10-15% of their revenues to sales, marketing and brand development. That is the typical investment they make to maintain and enhance their brand and their sales performance in the marketplace. You have a 45-60+ hour workweek. How much of that workweek, and how much of your income do you devote to the creation, enhancement and promotion of your brand?

As described in the previous chapter, your greatest contribution to yourself as a professional, and your biggest payback to yourself, comes in the form of the investment you make in your own professional development and the establishment of your brand. That investment should extend into promoting your brand. The value you offer your company, your employees, your customers, and ultimately, yourself, is predicated on the investment you are prepared to make in creating and promoting that value.

Your investment not only includes the skills and capabilities you develop to enhance your value, but also the development of your collateral. What collateral do you have that can reflect your brand? Collateral, such as your resume, articles you authored, or were quoted in, white papers? Those are examples of your brand collateral. Invest in your development, and the collateral that communicates your value.

What percentage of your time, what portion of your workweek is devoted to promoting your personal brand? Your accomplishments? Your results? Milestones? To what extent are you leveraging your network, your social media and other sources of outreach to ensure that the market knows who you are and the value you offer?

That is the investment you make in promoting your "Me" Enterprise.

Promote

Having assessed the marketplace, defined your personal brand, and made the investments to develop and cultivate your brand, you are ready to promote and position yourself for perpetual opportunities.

The concept of self-promotion is a delicate and fine art. We have all been taught at some point in our lives, not to "blow our own horn." So, our examination of promoting your value and expertise will be done in the context of promoting your brand, with minimal requirements to blow your own horn. That is the art . . . an art mastered by many corporations, and can be mastered by you.

Companies typically promote their brand in two ways: through deliberate, overt marketing efforts, such as television and print advertising, showroom displays and corporate sponsorships; and through less direct, subtler methods, such as hosting golf tournaments, underwriting charities, or supporting popular causes.

While deliberate marketing and promotional methods are more obvious in corporations, subtle forms of branding, though less obvious, can be equally impactful, as they can for your brand promotion strategy.

In the past, during times when employees and leaders remained in place with the same company for years, individual brands and reputations were established and perpetuated, many times unconsciously. Leaders knew employees through their experiences working together over the years, and likewise, employees knew each other. Individual reputations or brands, for better or worse, were established at the water cooler or through informal conversations based on those experiences.

In today's more virtual work environment, where in some cases, employees, leaders and teams reside in remote and different locations, and in some cases, never meet face-to-face, personal reputations and brands are created through subtler means. How you conduct yourself or how you engage others on a conference call, the tone and substance of your emails or other corporate communications, subtly, but distinctively, contribute to the creation and perpetuation of your brand.

As both methods, deliberate and subtle, are essential elements of corporate brand promotion strategies, they should be for you as well.

What direct or deliberate means can you employ to promote and make your capabilities and expertise known in the marketplace? Also, what more subtle, more indirect efforts can you employ to do the same? And in doing so, how can you employ these techniques without creating the perception or the reputation as a braggart or a self-promoter?

There are many recommendations that can be found for promoting one's self, in leadership books, management courses, the web and other sources. From our own experiences and from discussions with many successful leaders, we have extracted ten key elements that we believe can generate the greatest return in your efforts to promote your capabilities and value, all without blowing your own horn. And each of these principles will incorporate two fundamental themes:

- Self-promotion is not about promoting you, but about promoting the value you bring to others;

  and,

- "To receive, you must give . . ."

With those themes in mind, consider the following:

1 – Define and Articulate Your Value

The foundation of a corporation's marketing and promotion strategy is to (a) define the value their products and services provide to their customers, and (b) formulate a concise way to articulate that value, typically referred to in corporate speak as a "value proposition."

The foundation of promoting your value to your employer is

no different. Question #1 is: "What is the most significant value I offer my employer, my boss, my customers, that differentiates me from other prospective leaders?"

Does your value come in the form of generating or enhancing revenues? Reducing operating costs? Improving operational efficiencies? Developing products or services? Ensuring compliance? Wherever, and in whatever form your greatest value lies, determine as specifically as possible what you can offer your employer that is essential to the success of the company, and that few if any others can offer.

Once determined, Question #2 is "How do I articulate that value in a concise and compelling way?"

Corporations endlessly train their sales and marketing teams to articulate their value propositions or "elevator pitch," which concisely summarizes the value and benefits of their company's products and services. Employees must be proficient at delivering their company's elevator pitch so it does not sound contrived or rehearsed, but simply flows as part of the conversations and discussions they have with their customers about the company.

To what extent do you have, or can you create your own elevator pitch that communicates your value and your ambition to a prospective hiring executive in a concise and compelling manner?

Once you have your value proposition formulated, test it. Test it with trusted members of your network. Get honest feedback. Repeat it again, get more feedback, smooth out the wrinkles, and make your value proposition a smooth, comfortable part of your conversation with others. Ensure that your elevator pitch is both compelling and natural. Make it a concise statement of the value you bring to prospective employers, and a reflection of your brand.

2 – Define Your Target Audience

Once you are comfortable with your message, you are ready to identify your targeted prospective employers and create the opportunity to communicate your message. You are ready to seek out your next boss (even though he or she may not yet know that they are your next boss), and make it clear why they want, even need you, on their team. Be proud, be confident and be assertive in communicating why you are essential to your (next) company's success.

Within your current circumstance, targeting means knowing the pathway, or pathways, you would like to take in pursuit of your next position, be they within your existing company, with another company, or as an entrepreneur; and knowing the decision makers and influencers on that path.

If your career path lies within your own company, the question to be answered is, "Who are the decision makers and influencers on that path?" Typically, the answer is your boss, your boss's boss and your boss's colleagues.

If your career advancement pursuits are not within, but outside your current company, your targets are more likely to be recruiters, your customers or even your competitors. Think about how you can apply the same principles to a targeted external audience?

Finally, if your career interests lie in a more entrepreneurial direction, such as starting your own business or engaging in a start-up venture, the same techniques can be equally effective, even though your target audience may be different. In this case, your focus may be entrepreneurial forums, venture capitalists, investment groups, leadership forums or, franchising networks.

Whatever and wherever your career pursuit objectives are aimed, carefully and selectively target your efforts on those specific individuals best positioned to assist you in achieving those objectives, and find your deliberate and subtle ways of promoting your objectives.

3 – Assert Your Value Proposition

The key word in the above heading is "Assert"! A significant part of your value is your ability to actively and assertively create opportunities. There is no better place to employ this practice than with your own career. Your assertiveness is an essential component of your value proposition. You know who your prospective employers are; and actively and assertively create ways to engage them.

Asserting your value is not just about putting forth your idea and plan for your next job; it applies to your career as well. Make your ideas and your career plan known to your boss, your personal network and other key individuals who are in a position to help.

Just as we are told in medical circles that individuals can no longer simply rely on doctors, but must become responsible for their own healthcare, the same is true for our careers. Only you, not your company nor your boss, can drive your career plan. And that is true not just when you are unemployed and desperately looking a job. It should be happening with the same zeal, the same assertiveness, the same determination when you are working as when you are not.

For our executive mentioned at the beginning of this book, the words were still echoing in his head as returned from his Monday morning meeting . . .

"Our company just announced that our division has been sold. I do not yet know what this will mean for any of us. The next three to four weeks will be devoted to analyzing our team's *skills and capabilities and determining how they will fit in with the new company. All changes should be finalized within a month."*

After beating himself up for having been caught off guard from the surprise announcement and not being better prepared, he took a deep breath, gathered himself, and began to put together his game plan. He uploaded his resume, and began to update it. He pulled together a collection of documents that highlighted some of his recent accomplishments: newspaper articles about speaking engagements, an award he'd received at a Rotary Conference, a white paper he had written on emerging technologies, a PowerPoint presentation of his most recent business plan. He organized the documents into a portfolio.

He called his boss and asked if he could be the first of his boss's direct reports to meet. He asked for permission to meet with his boss's boss. He called one of his former colleagues, who had left the company to join a competitor to meet for lunch. His emotions went from shock and unnerved, to experiencing an adrenalin rush. He was determined to recover from being knocked back on his heels, to getting in front of the situation. He was determined to take charge. He wondered why he had not taken these actions before now, and made a mental note to himself, to be doing these things all the time, not just when things were uncertain and he was at risk of losing his job.

The benefits of proactively asserting your value proposition are many. The most important is that you minimize your risk of being caught off guard and unprepared. Additionally, your actions garner respect, from your bosses, from your colleagues and from your network. Third, you know where you stand in terms of your preparedness and marketability. Your network will point out weaknesses and shortcomings they see in your profile that you need to work on and improve.

Proactively and continuously assert your value proposition, and do so both when you are comfortably employed, and at times when you feel your situation is at risk. The result is, as the motto for the Boy Scouts says, you will "be prepared."

4 – Actively Engage Your Connections

Chapter 5's "Guiding Principles" section describes the critical role your network of mentors and trusted advisors play in guiding and supporting you and your career. Likewise, your network is an essential component of your promotion efforts. Most executives are in their current positions in part because of an introduction or sponsorship by one of their mentors who was part of their network. Chances are, your current role was made possible by a mentor or member of your network that made a timely introduction or referral.

As you consider this means of promotion, give consideration to those members of your network who will genuinely and actively support your career agenda. There are many advisors and mentors who will support your cause and root for you, but they may not be in the best position to make the best connection, or may not want to engage in an active role on your behalf. Use your network actively, but selectively.

5 – Sense, Intercept and Act on Negative Perceptions

There is a book entitled, "When Bad Things Happen to Good People." The professional equivalent of that adage is that, no matter how successful each of us may be, at times, we all experience failure and disappointment. We lose a deal that everyone expected us to win. We have a bad month, or a bad quarter or year. We fall short in completing a project. We fail to deliver against our forecast. Whatever the failure may have been, it not only impacted us, but someone else as well . . . including our boss, our boss's boss, and our company.

For example, at the same time Ian McKenzie, a senior sales executive in a European-based software company was having an introductory meeting with his new boss who had just come from another company, he was experiencing the worst financial quarter of his sales management career. His new boss had been told Ian was a top rate sales executive who consistently achieved or exceeded his sales goals. But that was precisely the one time in his career that he would not do so.

The sales executive knew that he must not allow his new boss to draw a negative perception of his sales performance based on this one outlier quarter. Ian took immediate steps to let his new boss know in advance the underperforming results he would soon see at the end of the quarter, and further explained the reasons for the poor performance, and the corrective actions that were being taken to ensure that his results would be back on track the following quarter.

There are often times and circumstances, beyond our financial or operational performance, when negative perceptions can be created about us, sometimes completely unbeknownst to us and based on the slightest of incidents.

Based on his financial performance, Mike Hudson was the most successful of twelve Regional Directors of a U.S.-based national financial services firm. For three consecutive years, his region enjoyed the top position in terms of revenues, profits and customer satisfaction. When an opening came up for his boss's position, however, Mike was told that he would not be considered for the position. When he asked why, he was told that he "was viewed as being overbearing and insensitive to his employees."

Surprised and confused by the characterization, he dug further to find that the characterization was born from a single incident regarding a female employee who was rebuffed when she wanted to discuss her pending maternity leave. Mike remembered the conversation, and remembered it coming at a bad time at the end of the fiscal quarter, and he also remembered asking if they could reschedule the discussion. Instead, viewing him as being unconcerned about her circumstance, the employee never rescheduled the meeting, but let it be known to others in the company that she was not happy with what she described as his "complete lack of sensitivity" for her situation.

Her characterization of the incident circulated among Mike's team, and ultimately to his boss, but was never communicated to him, until he inquired as to why he would not be considered for the promotional opportunity.

Perceptions, especially negative perceptions of you and your performance, are many times not communicated directly to you. In Mike Hudson's case, it was too late for him to take action to correct the perception.

In a manner similar to that of Mike Hudson, your operational and financial performance may be exceptional, but your career agenda still has the potential to be derailed or stalled for reasons you may never know. The burden of knowing how you are perceived, above and beyond tangible performance measures, lies with each of us. Your action is to cultivate your sensing devices, both verbal and non-verbal, and stay in tune with how you are perceived, by your employees, your peers and your employer, and to be prepared to take aggressive action to tackle and remedy any negative perceptions that exist.

Former New York City Mayor Ed Koch began every speech or public appearance among New York City constituents with the question, "How am I doing?" Know how you are doing, and be prepared to address the situation if the answer is not good.

6 – Actively Employ Social Media and Technology

Social media is emerging to become the predominant means of communicating, marketing and promoting business agendas. This is true among employers and recruiters alike. Accordingly, it must be an essential and active component of your career promotional efforts. Without getting into the virtues, advantages and/or limitations of one social media site over another, we simply offer two recommendations related to this medium:

1. Use it aggressively to promote your career; and

2. Use it wisely.

Social media is becoming the most powerful communications vehicle of our lifetime. However, it can also be the most damaging to our reputations, our brand, and our career if we are not careful. Everything you communicate is an extension of you and your brand. And once it is posted to the network, it is available to the universe and a part of your brand. Social media has the power to define and re-enforce who you are, what you stand for, and your career aspirations. Conversely, in an instant, it has the power to do just the opposite.

Every one of us has friends or colleagues that, under normal circumstances appear to exercise sound judgement about what they say, and to whom they say it. But then, out of the blue, they post a message on their favorite social media site that has political, religious or in some cases, sexual overtones, which makes us think, "What were they thinking?"

Use social media to the fullest extent of its power and its reach in creating, sustaining and enhancing your personal brand. But do so wisely. Before you hit the send button on any social media post, ask yourself one question: "Does this post reaffirm my brand, and enhance my career objectives?"

7 – OWN your Success, and make it visible!

In some cases, even when your work is absolutely essential to your customer's success, the work you do to sustain that success can be largely invisible, unless you make it so. That is even truer in a transient and virtual work environment. When people work at home, or work remotely, it is important not only to deliver good results, but also to ensure that you get recognized for achieving those results, by your employees, your boss, your company, and your customer.

There is an expression, "Success has a thousand fathers, failure is an orphan." In a virtual, transient world, successful results are typically the results of many individuals. Thus they are open and available to many people to claim as their own. Your task is to ensure that you are recognized for the results you achieve.

Are the results you achieve visible? To your bosses? Your customers?

Below is an example of the impact of visibility, from the earliest days of the computer era, but one that is still as relevant today as it was in the 1980's, especially in today's virtual workplace . . .

A computer services organization that was responsible for providing computer maintenance services to a leading financial services organization sent out its yearly customer survey to its client to assess their customer satisfaction levels. To its surprise and disappointment, the results were not satisfactory. Concerned that they could potentially lose a valuable client, the services company decided to take an "improve at any cost" approach to improving their scores. Their strategy was to choose the four lowest scores and aggressively take the actions required to improve in each category.

One of the four lowest-rated areas was in the area of preventive maintenance, which consisted of taking actions during off-hours to ensure systems were properly maintained, including changing filters, alignments, diagnostics, adjustments, etc. Given that their client was a financial services company and totally dependent on their computer services during business hours, preventive maintenance actions could only be accomplished during the 3rd shift, the midnight hours. The company felt this would be an area where they could easily improve their scores.

At the end of the following performance year, however, the company's preventive maintenance scores remained low. Confused by the lack of improvement in their scores in this area, the company sought feedback from their client to better understand why, after taking aggressive actions to improve their scores, the results continued to lag. What they discovered was that, even though their preventive maintenance actions had indeed improved, because the actions were taken during off hours, they were invisible to their client, and in some cases, even to their first shift counterparts who were the primary point of contact with the client.

Understanding this lack of visibility, the company took the additional action, after each preventive maintenance operation, of sending their client a formal letter detailing the nature and extent of the actions that were taken the previous evening. As a result, the following year, the company received its highest scores in the area of preventive maintenance.

The company learned an invaluable lesson – delivering results is insufficient, if there is no corresponding recognition for delivery of those results. After learning this valuable lesson, the company changed its motto from "deliver quality results" to **"VISIBLY** deliver quality results!"

Similarly, your visibility should extend beyond your boss or your customer, out into the marketplace. How do you make yourself visible to prospective companies or employers outside of your current job? The answer is primarily through three means . . . write, publish and present.

"Of course he's an expert. He wrote a book!"

"An expert is someone who speaks to an audience about a particular topic . . . and the audience pays attention."

"I worked at my craft for more than thirty years, and it seemed like I was the only person that knew what I was doing. Then I presented my paper at a conference, and suddenly, I'm an expert."

There is perhaps no more effective means of establishing and promoting your personal brand than to write, publish and speak.

Whether it is writing a book, a technical paper, a newspaper article, a blog, or simply finding opportunities to be quoted, having your name on or associated with a byline is an essential element in branding. Writing also is the springboard to speaking. If you want to increase your odds of getting in front of a live audience to espouse your favorite topic, and your expertise in that topic, write and publish on that topic. Your market and your professional brand increase exponentially every time you write and publish on a topic related to your brand, and every time you speak to an audience regarding that topic.

8 – Give Back

As cited in the section in Chapter 5, "The Guiding Principles of the "Me" Enterprise, "giving back" is not just about doing the right thing, but is perhaps one of the most effective means of promoting your personal brand. If you accept as one of the laws of the universe that "as you give, you shall receive," then as you give to your company, to your community, to others, your brand is enriched far beyond what you give. Giving back is the preventive medicine that fosters "yes" when others ask about you, and the results inhibit "no."

The concept of giving back, in this context, is not about giving money, but giving of your time, your talent, yourself. Beyond your day-to-day responsibilities, what can you offer your company, or your employees, as a way of giving back? And the same question can be asked about your community. Whether through civic organizations, your local community college or tech school or private entities, what talent and experience can you offer that will help others succeed? Find the answer. And experience the joy of "doing well, by doing good."

Giving back is about the joy of giving to others. It is about helping others succeed, and is done in the truest spirit of giving. And though it is not about what you get in return, giving back promotes good will that pays endless dividends for you and your career. Giving back promotes the positive in you, and about you.

9 - Promote the Accomplishments of Others

An adjunct to the concept of giving back is the concept of promoting the accomplishments and successes of others. To paraphrase Newton's law, "every action creates a reaction."

Every success you have achieved, and will achieve, is in part, a direct result of someone else's influence or actions. Promote them and celebrate their contributions to your success openly and often. You will strengthen your relationship and good will with them, which will only encourage and motivate them to take an even more active role in your success.

In some eastern cultures, when having dinner in a restaurant with guests, it is impolite, for example, when having wine, to refresh your own glass. If you want to top off your wine glass, instead, top off the glass of one of your guests. He or she, in turn, will reciprocate and refresh yours.

Take a page from this concept in your efforts to promote your career agenda and employ the principle, "If you want the light to shine on you, shine it on others!" Promote and celebrate your boss, your colleagues, your employees, your customers, your partners; and in turn, your career aspirations will be the better for it.

10 – Timing

In real estate, the mantra is "location, location, location." In promotion, it is about "timing, timing, timing."

> On the cover of their October 2008 issue, Smart Money Magazine declared, "Double Your Nest Egg: Now is the Time to Jump Into Cheap Stocks!"

The problem is the issue came out September 16, 2008, the very day the stock market started its worst drop since the Great Depression. The Dow Jones, which was 11,500 when the issue came out, subsequently dropped to as low as 8,200, nearly a 30% drop. At the time, Smart Money Magazine had no way of knowing how bad its timing would be. But consequently, their reputation and credibility took a significant hit as a result of their ill-timed cover.

As you consider your efforts to promote your career agenda, take pause to consider the timing of any of your promotional efforts. If your company or division is doing well . . . your timing is good. If growth is spawning the creation of a new division within your company, your timing is good.

In contrast, if your company or division recently recorded poor results, or is performing poorly, consider that this may not be the ideal time to promote your agenda.

You will not always be able to predict or anticipate good or bad timing, but it is essential that you consider the "when" of your promotional efforts, as well as the what, the how and the who of those efforts.

One other very important aspect to consider regarding timing is that this process is far more powerful when you already have a job, rather than when you wait until you are out of work. There is an expression that goes, "The best time to position yourself for a new job, is when you have a job. The worst time is when you don't."

*   *   *

On occasion, the collective virtues and benefits of promoting one's self can converge in a single act. Consider the act of a talented, determined employee who knew her value, knew the benefits she could achieve for her company, and knew she had to take matters into her own hands to make it happen.

Her boss, Geoffrey Miller, CEO of a growing Dallas, Texas-based technology company, loves to tell her story which occurred when he was speaking at a user's conference . . .

At the reception following the CEO's talk, one of my employees that I did not know at the time, approached me to ask if she could have a few minutes of my time. I agreed, and in a matter of two minutes, she proceeded to outline for me a very succinct, but comprehensive career plan she had developed for herself that included very specific ways she could add value to our company. She was sensitive to the spontaneous and unplanned nature of our conversation, and asked if she could arrange a time to meet with me and explain her thoughts in greater detail. Intrigued by the boldness of her actions, and the thoughtfulness of her plan, I could not resist.

A week later, we met in my office, along with her manager whom she had invited. In our meeting, in greater detail than our earlier meeting, she laid out a very specific career plan for herself, and included equally specific ideas as to the contributions she believed she could make to our company. And to top it off, she was very bold in asking each of us for our support in her achieving her plan. Overwhelmed by her initiative, we both agreed to support her career plan. After the employee left, her manager and I were left to marvel at the woman's thoughtfulness and assertiveness in communicating exactly what she wanted, and how it would benefit us. We commented that we needed a hundred more employees just like her.

"Her business ideas" said Miller, "were ideas neither I nor anyone on our management team had ever thought about, and more importantly, she had the courage to seek the opportunity to present her ideas to me."

Miller later shared that the employee is now running a profitable business practice which is generating growth, he said, that the company would have never otherwise realized.

"I have used her as the poster child for courage and creativity in every management and employee meeting I have. I often wonder what we could be as a company if ten more employees came forward the way she did!"

*   *   *

While there is no exclusivity in these principles, they are, however, a distillation of tried and proven methods, as cited by many successful corporate professionals for promoting your career and your career agenda.

There are many other examples and techniques that you can find from other sources, including your own experiences. And we, like you, continue to explore other methods, both deliberate and subtle, where you can promote your brand and your career agenda. From social media to speaking engagements to involvement in civic clubs, or other work and community related activities, all are branding activities, and all should be put to use.

Promote, promote, promote. . . ..

Repeat:

Assess, Define, Invest, Promote, and then. . . . Repeat!

The graphic at the beginning of this chapter illustrates that the art of positioning or marketing your career aspirations and agenda to prospective employers is an iterative, non-ending process. The circumstances that got you to your current position were different than the circumstances that will get you to your next position. You recognize that your circumstances and the marketplace are continually changing, and that you must continually re-assess your skills, your position in the market, and your brand, and make the changes necessary to adapt to those conditions.

In the 1970's, the shelf life of a product's value and its usefulness to its customers was estimated to be 24-30 months. That was the average time a product or service could sustain customer revenues before being overtaken by newer and more effective versions, or needed to be enhanced. Today, that shelf life value is estimated to be less than six months.

It can be said that the effective brand of an employee's shelf life is comparable. With changes in technology, market conditions, competitive positioning and skills, the "Me" Enterprise does not and cannot rely on what has worked up to now.

All that was done in the creation and promotion of your brand is recognized as an ongoing, iterative process. . . . a process of continually re-assessing the market, re-thinking your brand in light of changing market conditions, re-branding your skills and capabilities to match those conditions, and re-writing and re-promoting those skills to the market.

In summary, positioning is about how you position and market yourself in support of your career agenda and aspirations. How will you know when you're doing it right? When prospective employers begin to seek you out and pursue *you*, instead of you pursuing *them*.

Outcomes

Blueprint for the 'Me' Enterprise

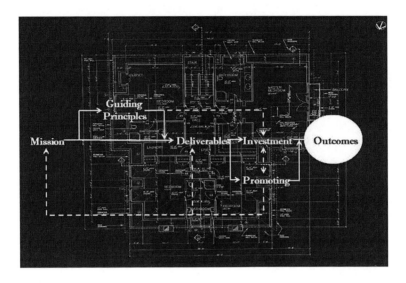

"If you're an employee, behave like an entrepreneur. If you're an entrepreneur, behave like an employee."

In executing each of the steps in *The "Me" Enterprise" Blueprint: its Mission, its Principles, its Deliverables, and its Positioning*, the logical questions to be asked are, "What are the outcomes to be expected? What are the benefits to you, the employee? And for your employer, the Corporation that serves as your customer?

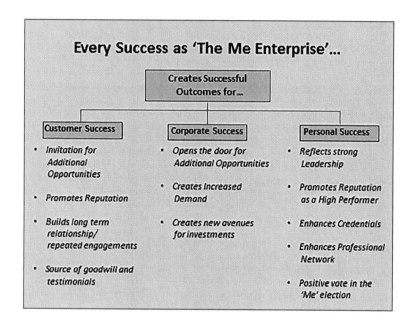

While operating within this framework offers no guarantees of absolute certainty, history provides overwhelming evidence, supported by the views of some of industry's most innovative and successful leaders, that the results or outcomes are significant, and can be typically characterized in four categories:

High Performance "Me" Enterprise – At its most fundamental level, evidence shows that the core ingredients of the "Me" Enterprise concept significantly increases your ability to survive in the tumultuous and continually changing business climate of digitization and disruption.

Beyond increasing your ability to merely survive in today's business climate, there is yet additional evidence that suggests employing the ingredients of the "Me" Enterprise positions you to excel in that climate.

Corporate or Customer Success – As stated in the "Operating Principles" outlined in Chapter 7, "Your success is ultimately measured by your customer's success." Using that measure, evidence further shows that those who embrace and employ the principles of the "Me" Enterprise deliver improved value and results to the Corporation they serve.

PART III

The Role of the Corporation

"I get it, but do you think the folks in headquarters get it?"

Chapter 7

The Silent Killers of Corporate Productivity (and Individual Careers)

IN THE HIGHFLYING days of the dot.com boom, corporate revenues and profits soared and any issues companies had regarding productivity were in many cases masked by the bulging top and bottom lines on the balance sheet. As one CEO explained, "When the GDP was in excess of 4%, we didn't spend a whole lot of time worrying about fine tuning our cost models."

In leaner times, however, when revenues are harder to come by, competition is more intense, margins are thinner and the GDP is closer to 2%, productivity issues tend to get more attention.

Though technological innovations continue to drive new growth, there are few signs that the high flying days of the dot.com boom will ever come back on the horizon anytime soon. Digitization has led to the greatest surge in corporate productivity and efficiencies in the history of commerce.

New technologies, combined with restructuring, downsizing, mergers, acquisitions and other actions, have helped achieve significant improvements in efficiencies and corporate margins. However, the productivity needle appears to be stuck around or below 2%.

With competition remaining as fierce as ever, corporations continue to search for additional improvements in their productivity and their performance. While it appears that at least a measure of those improvements can be found in the principles of the "Me" Enterprise, many corporations continue to inadvertently employ practices that thwart growth and improvements to productivity.

Today the cost of leadership in a corporation is approximately 35-50% of the total cost of its workforce, and rising. In their efforts to reduce these costs, corporations have automated many functions, outsourced many functions, reduced their leadership ranks, reorganized and restructured their organizations. Yet they continue to employ practices that are drags on productivity. Many of these practices are assumed to be essential, and many are. The way they are carried out, however, and who carries them out, tends to inhibit productivity and, at the same time has the potential to turn talented and valuable leaders into glorified administrators.

The next frontier of productivity is reorienting business practices and leadership roles and drawing a sharper distinction between customer- oriented responsibilities and administrative responsibilities.

While there is growing evidence of companies quickly transitioning their culture and practices to today's fast paced, technologically driven economy, there is comparable evidence of company practices that continue to impede rather than enhance productivity. These practices remain commonplace in many corporations, and are viewed by many executives as "good ideas gone wrong." These practices are the other side of the corporate productivity coin, which one executive called "the silent killers of corporate productivity."

Beyond the gains that continue to be realized by automating back office functions, and the reductions associated with outsourcing, workforce reductions, restructuring and redeployments, the next frontier of productivity lies in how effectively corporations are able to reduce, if not eliminate what has come to be known as the "internal abyss," practices and activities that consume a growing percentage of a leader's time and energy, thus reducing their effectiveness in their performance as value-added, customer-focused leaders.

What are some of the practices, and there are many, that are commonplace and viewed as essential to a company's day-to-day operations, but silently, almost imperceptibly, rob a company and its leaders of valuable time, attention and energy, thus making it and them less productive, and less competitive? What follows is a small sampling of those practices. These examples of practices are put forth not to argue that they are non-essential and should be eliminated, but with the intent to question how they are done, and by whom.

Further, it is argued that none of these "silent killers of productivity," collectively referred to as the "internal abyss," singlehandedly destroy corporate productivity or individual leader's careers. But collectively, silently and inadvertently, they take leadership time, attention and focus away from the customer, and toward internal issues that could be resolved in better ways.

In contrast to the practices that enhance the productivity of corporations in the era of digitization, these are a sampling of what have come to be known as the "silent killers of corporate productivity," or the "internal abyss."

The Internal Abyss

> **"Internal Abyss"** (n) – A phenomenon, typically found in corporations, in which leaders whose primary value to their company is their customer facing expertise, are gradually lulled into taking on more administrative responsibilities, thus reducing their individual competitive edge and value to their customer, and to their company.

Timothy Palmer was described as an IT security whiz kid. He founded a successful startup business specializing in Internet security, which in less than three years of operations, had surpassed $40 million in annual revenues, was operating at a profit, and was on a trajectory of exponential growth. Predictably, Palmer's company was acquired by one of the leading global IT companies, and integrated into the new company's services organization. Palmer was regarded as one of the top technical minds in the industry. He was excellent in front of customers, and had agreed to head his new company's global IT security practice.

During the six months of negotiations prior to being acquired, Palmer had all but abandoned his customer work to concentrate on preparing for and making presentations and negotiating with his new company. Once the acquisition was successfully concluded, Palmer continued to spend the majority of his time on internal meetings with different business units within his new company, presenting the capabilities and strategies of his new practice. Months passed and Palmer continued to find himself devoting more and more of his time to making internal presentations on the strategy and performance of his practice, and less and less time doing what he loved and was best at – meeting and negotiating with customers.

Before the end of his first year as the Global Security Practice

Leader for his new firm, frustrated and disillusioned by the changing nature of his role, Palmer resigned his position, left and started a new company.

Timothy Palmer and the global IT giant that acquired his company had fallen victim to the "internal abyss," a condition where a talented content expert gets lulled into doing more internally focused administrative work, and spending less time performing more valuable, customer oriented activities.

The "internal abyss" is one that many companies, large and small, fall victim to. Slowly, almost imperceptibly, leaders, who are the company's most vital assets in terms of delivering value to customers, spend more of their time and efforts performing internal, administrative tasks, thus robbing their company of their primary value, which is working face to face with customers, thereby resulting in them becoming very expensive, glorified administrators.

The internal abyss is not something that corporations design into their management model. Corporations don't purposely intend their leaders to perform non-value added activities; nor do they intend to rob them of their time doing customer facing work. It just happens. Slowly, imperceptibly, it just happens.

Emily Braxton, the only female Regional VP, was regarded by her peers as perhaps the best of all of the Regional VP's for a telecommunications provider. She described her frustrations:

We (her company) have been very aggressive in adapting new technologies. We use CRM (Customer Relationship Management) software to track all of our sales and operational activities with every customer. We know who has talked to whom. We know what was said, and what next steps and actions are required on every deal we do. We know the revenue history of every customer, and every vital contact inside every one of our customers' organizations. Pretty good, right?

The problem is, every ounce of new intelligence we gather through our technology, our headquarters organization wants yet another incremental report. They have the same data we have. They can analyze it as well as we can. But in addition, they want reports from us, providing them our interpretation of the data. And they want to have more conference calls to discuss the reports. And at the same time, I'm expected to be on top of everything that is going on in my region. They keep adding, but they never take away. I can't remember the last time I spent an entire day meeting with my sales team and with customers.

Thus the paradox of technology . . . Whereas we expect technology to eliminate or reduce the administrative workload of team leaders, in many cases, it does just the opposite. Not because of the technology, but because of the way executive management teams use the technology.

As corporations incorporate more technologies, they have begun to create massive amounts of information, all intended to improve corporate productivity and competitiveness. Yet, in many cases, just the opposite occurs. Leaders are pulled into more and more internal meetings and discussions, and as a result, more and more into the "internal abyss."

The result is a slow, almost undetectable drain on corporate and leadership productivity, and it comes in the form of many activities. As you read the following examples, ask yourself two questions:

1. How much time do I spend on this type of activity in a given week?

2. In what other ways could this function be performed, that would be more efficient, and create less drain on a leader's time and energy?

The Meeting and Conference Call Sinkhole

You are sitting in on your third of five mandatory conference calls that you participate in each week, in support of your various business units and projects. During the call, a question is directed to one of the attendees by the call moderator. And after a slight pause, the respondent says, "Can you please repeat the question?"

The individual to whom the question was directed, did not hear the question the first time, because they, like you and most everyone else on the call, had the call on mute, was doing email, or having a side conversation, or some other task that was more vital or important to them in the moment than sitting in on a mandatory conference call. Most of the attendees have little or no input or value to add to the call, but it is one of several mandatory calls that consume between 10 and 20 hours of their time each week.

Weekly and sometimes daily mandatory conference calls and meetings have become a staple of today's corporate culture, and will continue to do so for the foreseeable future. Some analysts estimate that 30, 40 and even 50% of corporate leaders' activities are consumed preparing for, attending or taking action items from events which do not directly apply to them, or to which they can offer little or any direct value.

But the manner in which most corporations employ conference calls, they have also become a growing part of the "administrative abyss."

What if conference call announcements were accompanied by a message from the call organizer that said:

"Please be on this call only if you have information that needs to be communicated to the team, or IF the information that will be discussed on the call is vital to your current responsibilities. Otherwise, following the call, please read and confirm your understanding of the minutes to ensure that you are current on the status of our team performance. Please contact me if you have any questions."

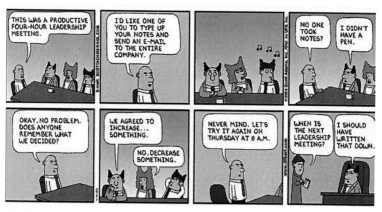

© UFS, Inc.

What if the same caveat was included in announcements of all meetings? Or management updates? Or the many other daily corporate activities that can easily fall into the "internal abyss?"

The Cascading Town Hall

The quarterly results have been announced. The CEO conducts a town hall meeting to announce the results and outline the company's strategy going forward. Given the multiple divisions, business units and layers of leadership within the corporation, for the next 3-4 weeks following the announcement, every division and business unit leader will spend hours preparing and presenting the same results to their constituency that the CEO presented in the initial town meeting.

Employees will be presented the same information, in many instances on multiple occasions, with little or no incremental content or messaging that helps them perform their jobs any more effectively.

How much time and effort is devoted by corporate leaders to these types of activities? How much, if any, incremental information or value is provided? How much redundancy is inherent in these activities? How can this information be provided once, without the multiple, redundant downstream repeats of the same information?

The Escalation Escalator

A highly valued customer has raised a technical issue with their Corporate Account Manager, which, given the nature of the issue and the customer, was quickly communicated to the CEO. There are two technical groups, and five layers of management that this issue touches . . . which means, in addition to the technical talent that is pulled in to correct the problem, there are seven layers of leadership in the corporation directly engaged in this issue.

Given the visibility of this issue, all seven group managers drop what they are doing to "stay on top of" this issue. All seven layers of leaders are cascading and exchanging information, ostensibly to ensure that the issue is properly resolved.

Customer fire drills such as the above are a powerful magnetic draw into the "internal abyss." Given the desire and expectation to be "in the know" or to be viewed as "on top of things," anyone who is remotely involved in matters of high visibility within a corporation wants to demonstrate their commitment to getting the problem solved. The reality is, only one or a few individuals are actively engaged in solving the problem, while multiple corporate leaders devote countless hours to either being informed or passing updates and information up and down the corporate ladder.

One CEO derisively referred to this phenomenon as "the Ronald McDonald School of Management." "In their eagerness to be viewed as part of the solution," he says laughingly, "everyone puts on a red wig and wears outlandish clothing to be seen even though they have nothing to do with the quality of hamburgers."

When asked what he does to prevent this from happening in his company, he says:

> "We have a simple rule: When a customer issue gets escalated to my office and I have to get involved, I direct all other managers to stand down and continue doing their jobs, and I will handle it. If I need them, I will call them. Otherwise, just keep doing your job, and my Admin will keep you informed."

The Performance Appraisal Parade

At the start of the new fiscal year, you and your manager produced your annual performance plan, which included a series of goals and expectations that you would be expected to meet during the upcoming year. As the year progressed, you were assigned to five different projects, and reported to six different direct and indirect bosses, only one of whom was vaguely aware of your performance plan and expectations, none of which related to the projects in which you were actually engaged. With the year coming to an end, it is annual review time. All of the managers that you were responsible to over the past year are expected to have input to your annual review, but none of their inputs correlated to your original plan, nor to the work you are expected to perform in the coming year.

To satisfy the administrative requirement, your manager asks you to write up something that would serve as input for your review; and then scheduled time to go over your review (70% of which was written by you). This activity is performed on multiple occasions by each manager, for each of their employees. As a result, employees begin to see the entire process as a farcical exercise in bureaucracy.

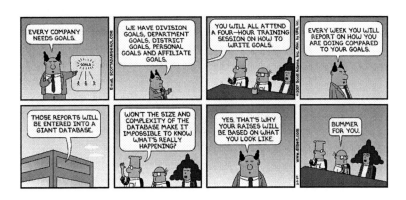

Performance appraisals are an essential component of employee and corporate performance and productivity. Additionally, they are a foundational element of every company's culture and behavior. There is a growing recognition, however, that the traditional practice of how employee appraisals are conducted is becoming an anachronism, and counter-productive to the goals they hope to achieve.

The CEO Visit

A visit by the CEO is a month out, and is considered a "big deal" to the local subsidiary. The Subsidiary Manager wants to make a good impression, and has instructed each of his managers to prepare a brief ten-minute presentation to be made to the CEO. To ensure their readiness, he conducts twice weekly reviews to get a status update on and to rehearse their preparations. Each presentation will include an update on their respective business highlights, and the Subsidiary Manager wants to ensure that each delivers just the right message. The CEO is completely unaware that the Subsidiary's leadership team has devoted up to 30% of their time and effort over the past month in preparing for a two-day executive visit.

An executive visit to a local division, country or business unit is generally regarded as a good thing. It serves as a morale boost for the local group, and gives the executive an up-close view of the business. However, on most occasions like this, it turns into a significant undertaking of management time and effort to provide the visiting executive what will be a scripted and artificial view of the true nature of the local business.

What if, instead of what one Country manager refers to as "preparing to host the Olympics" the CEO's visit includes not pre-announced meetings, but spontaneous, more impromptu meetings with local managers? That way, the executive not only gets a more accurate, less scripted view of the state of the local business, but he or she also gets a better feel for which of the local managers truly knows the state of their business.

More impromptu, more spontaneous and less scripted meetings for what many regard as "ceremonial" executive visits, also eliminates countless hours of management preparation, saved from the "administrative abyss."

Customer Visits

As Samantha Atkins arrived for her weekly Monday morning leadership meeting, she noticed the #1 item on the agenda was "Customer Visits." As her Division head began the meeting, he explained that at the recently held offsite executive retreat, the company CEO expressed concerns that the company was drifting too far away from its customers. As a result, it was agreed that the company would institute a mandatory executive customer visit program in which each Division Leadership team would be issue a list of customers that they were to visit each month, with feedback reports submitted directly to the CEO on each of those visits.

The belief was that mandatory customer visits by company executives would demonstrate an increased level of corporate commitment to that customer, and in turn, create an increase in customer satisfaction, and revenues.

Is that really the case? Discussions with many account executives suggest just the opposite.

"First of all," states Mike Bittman, a Senior Account Executive who has account responsibilities for a European based electronics manufacturer, "customers understand the "Corporate Visit" game. They get it. They do it themselves for *their* customers. They go along with it, but it rarely has a positive impact on our account performance. If we want corporate visits to mean something, arrange them when we have a problem that needs to be solved, or an issue that needs to be escalated, or a proposal that we are having difficulty closing. Other than that, they are a waste of our time and the customers, and take significant time from our account team to arrange and coordinate."

A Senior VP who headed up the Consulting Services Division in Asia Pacific for a US based IT company entertained a steady parade of corporate visitors from his company's headquarters; and each visitor wanted to include a customer visit as part of their Hong Kong itinerary. Customer visits were a standard checklist item for visiting executives, followed by detailed trip reports back to their headquarters organization regarding the customer that was visited, and the outcome of their discussions. The visits were intended to re-enforce the company's declared commitment to being "customer focused."

The reality was, in many cases, quite different. An international corporate visit, just for the sake of introductions and "How's our account team doing?" conversations is a major logistical undertaking, and provides little or no insights or ideas for meaningful improvement as it relates to the company's performance.

"In many cases", the executive said, "we had to literally beg customers for their time for these visits. And by the way we were not the only one - other vendors were requesting the same. One of our customers jokingly said they will need to invest in a special team dedicated to doing nothing but hosting corporate visitors from the US."

Ceremonial customer visits, be they local or international, are not customer work. In fact, they are more times than not, significant detractors from customer work. They are another example of the "administrative abyss." Customer visits are value added and meaningful only when and if they provide the customer and the account team the power of the visiting executive's position to solve a problem; or knowledge and experience that can add value to the customer's business or operational objectives; or achieve a resolution of issues that result in additional opportunities and customer success.

As a corporate executive, an effective way to judge the power and the value of customer visits is when account teams are seeking you out to come in and meet with their customer to solve problems or generate additional opportunities. Customer visits should be a "pull" activity, and not a "push" activity. When pushed, customer visits detract; when pulled, the company, the account team and the customer are on track to achieve even greater successes together.

The Data Dump (GIGO – "Garbage In, Garbage Out")

The world of digitization is a world that has come to be governed by data. Most companies have incorporated the elements of data mining and data analysis into virtually every aspect of their organization. Yet the disciplines and processes by which data is gathered in many companies is suspect, with minimal oversights. The outcome of a lack of discipline in what is viewed as a critical element of a company's operation results in productivity losses, misaligned strategies and missed opportunities.

A top tier IT professional services firm in the US requires each of its consultants to submit a weekly report called the "LAR" (Labor Activity Report). The LAR tells the company how many employees are deployed to which customer projects; what skills are required for those projects; what customers, including type, size and vertical sectors, are hiring their consultants; the length of each engagement; the hourly fee being billed to the customer and the average charge rate.

The reports are an essential element in determining skill requirements, hiring activities, customer deployments and other vital aspects of the company's operations. New employees spend one full day of their new employee orientation program learning the LAR system and the importance of the labor reporting process. Further, they are directed, with the full wrath of the company coming down on them should they fail, to deliver their LAR's not later than 5:00 PM each Thursday afternoon. The weekly LAR report was deemed to be the highest priority of a consultant's weekly activities.

Based on data analyzed from the reports over the previous quarter, the company was experiencing exceptionally utilization rates in the financial services sector, suggesting that there would be a need to hire additional consultants to respond to the coming demand. Upon further analysis, however, the management team realized that the revenues had not matched the high utilization rates that the LAR data indicated. Higher utilization would indicate higher revenues, but that was not the case. Something was amiss.

Perplexed by the discrepancy, management conducted an internal audit of the reporting process to assess the veracity of the data coming from the reports, and get to the bottom of the discrepancy.

The audit findings revealed, among other things, that the consultants" primary focus in completing their LAR reports was getting the reports in on time, by end of day each Thursday. This objective overshadowed the objective of submitting accurate data. Given a typical 14-16 hour workday left precious little time to create the LAR's. They found that most LAR's were being filled out either at midnight on Wednesday evenings, or at the end of the day on Thursday, while on a plane or on a customer site. Neither of those occasions allowed for a quality report, and knowing company's emphasis in submitting the reports on time, on many occasions, the consultants would include "estimates" of their time allocations and client projections. The practice of "estimating", the audit revealed, was a pervasive practice with many consultants, resulting in grossly underestimated or overestimated time projections for hiring needs and skills requirements, with little or no verification from the customer or from supervisors.

Had management not analyzed the quality of the data, it would have moved forward to hire additional consultants that, in reality, would not have been needed, and would have led to significant losses.

The lesson learned was one of a company placing more emphasis on "completing the report", with less emphasis on the quality of the information provided in the report. Reporting practices such as these are becoming more and more prevalent, with companies spending millions of dollars on the systems, the time and the effort required to perform them. With an investment such as this, it is essential that the quality of the data supersedes all other factors in management reporting.

As a Managing Principle of the firm stated, "GIGO! Faulty intelligence is worse than no intelligence at all. If there is no integrity in the process, there is no integrity in the data."

The Technology (non) Savant

Eric Caputo, a corporate Vice President and head of his company's Administrative Services group had the reputation of making great presentations in corporate meetings. From PowerPoint, to Excel, to Word documents, to WordPress, to Trello, Bitrix, they were all embedded in his presentations, and they all had the look and feel and the content of a professional production house. His secret . . . He didn't know how to use any of those tools; but he knew who did.

Eric Caputo, though he was (and remains) a technological illiterate, knew every executive assistant on the fourth floor, and many on the 3rd and 5th floors, and he knew each one's mastery of different technology tools; and he cultivated relationships with each one.

Some of the staff that he regularly called on to assist him in his presentations worked in his group, so he had no compunction about recruiting them for his presentation projects. Others worked for different groups, but were reluctant to say "no" when a Vice President comes calling. All of them, however, had other tasks to perform, other projects to complete, and other bosses to support. Though each could argue "not my job", they did not. The result for Eric was a reputation for giving great presentations. The result for the company was lost productivity.

Every employee knows an Eric Caputo. Someone who not only doesn't know, but refuses to learn even the most fundamental technology tools, and up to now, has managed to survive their ignorance. But that phenomenon won't last for long . . . not if William Scearce has his way.

Scearce is the founder and senior partner of a multi-practice law firm, and for anyone who does not know, legal presentations, court documents, judicial decrees and client proposals are the Mother's milk of a law firm's business. When preparing to expand the firm in 2013, Scearce made a decision that all lawyers and paralegal professionals that joined his firm would have the technology skills to produce their own documents. Each new hire, as part of their employment agreement, signed a document that said they either possessed the skills, or would acquire them through training that the firm paid for, before the conclusion of their probationary period.

There are those in every company, large and small, that professes to be technologically ignorant, and some wear it as a badge of honor. In reality, they are a drag on productivity, and more and more companies are going the route of William Scearce . . . you either have it, or you will get it. But one way or the other, you will be responsible for your own TC (technology quotient).

The Perpetual Edict of Expense Controls

Every company goes through a bad stretch, when revenues are lagging expenses, and cash flow is tight. That is typically when companies institute companywide expense controls ranging from restrictions on travel, meetings, capital expenditures, and even office supplies. The perpetual edict of expense controls is issued typically on a blanket basis, independent of the nature or the critical need for the expense. Some of those expenses are required for customer or revenue generating activities, which is exactly what companies need to address in times of cash flow issues.

It was week eleven of the thirteen-week quarter when Mike Andrews received the expense controls memo, including a ban on all travel until the end of the quarter. Mike's sales team had several deals pending that were included in the company's quarterly revenue forecast, but knew he would have a difficult time closing them over the phone. His sales reps needed to be in front of their customers, especially as the quarter was in its final weeks.

After discussions with his Division VP and CFO, he was able to get an exception on the restriction, and later the company modified their expense control policy in recognition of the need to distinguish between random expenses and mission critical expenses.

Mike's questioning of the blanket expense control policy had a positive ending, both for him and his team, and for the company. The company changed their expense control policy from a "broad brush", across-the-board expense reduction edict, to one that provided a specific dollar amount or percentage reduction target, leaving cost center managers the discretion as to how to achieve those results without jeopardizing critical, customer facing activities that would have a detrimental effect on business.

Hopefully other companies will follow suit. The perpetual expense control edict, while well intended, sometimes can achieve the exact opposite of its desired intent.

*   *   *

These examples, cited by a range of executives as silent killers of corporate productivity are but a small slice of practices that were once deemed appropriate and productive, but perhaps have gone awry. There were many more examples, too many to detail in this segment, that tended to fall into the categories and activities listed below.

Given these categories of activities, what percentage of a leader's time and effort is dedicated to these types of activities? And how might these activities, if they are deemed essential, be performed in a more efficient way so as not to fall into the "internal abyss?" How can some of these activities, in their current and traditional form, be "Uberized" in order to improve the performance and productivity of a company's leaders, and in turn, the productivity, profitability and survival of the company itself?

Business Related Activities:

- Analyzing, preparing and reporting Profit and Loss statements on a weekly, monthly, quarterly and annual basis;

- Analyzing and reviewing performance metrics on a daily, weekly, monthly, quarterly and annual basis;

- Preparing Budgeting and Capital Spending initiatives, planning, preparing and seeking approvals;

- Preparing Restructuring or Organization Plans, and the multi-level reviews and approvals required.

Infrastructure Related Activities:

- Activities pertaining to securing and negotiating office space;

- Dealing with IT infrastructure proposals, projects and approvals;
- Reports and communications with the Headquarters of home office
- Activities pertaining to Communication Technology
- Administrative tasks associated with reviewing technology applications or other tools related matters

Employee Related Activities:

- Activities related to hiring, restructuring;
- Talent Mapping and workforce planning
- Exit Interviews
- Performance Appraisals
- Employee surveys
- Career Development, employee issues
- Compensation planning and approvals

Communications Activities:

- Town halls
- Ongoing employee communication
- Cross functional communications
- Morale boosting events

These activities are not put forth to argue that they should be eliminated, or that executives and other leaders should not be engaged in them. To the contrary, most are indeed necessary to a company's day-to-day operations and performance, and most, if not all, require executive and leadership actions. And while none, by themselves, represents a dramatic drain on leadership time and effort; nor by eliminating any one of them will they provide a significant increase in corporate productivity, all can be performed in ways that are more efficient, and by the individuals that are most suited to perform them.

Collectively, the way in which many companies currently execute these activities, they can indeed result in a drain on corporate productivity. It can be argued that these activities, if they indeed are critical functions, can be performed much more efficiently, in ways that do not take the company or its leaders into the internal abyss.

What is the percentage of management or leadership activities such as these are prevalent in your corporation? And in what better, more productive ways could that time, effort and brain power be used, to increase revenues and customer satisfaction, creating better products and services, and reducing costs in your corporation?

"Glorified Administrators"

In the same way these and other administrative practices impact corporate productivity, they can have a similar negative effect on the careers of individuals. The more time and effort leaders are forced to put into administrative activities, the less energy they apply to solving customer problems and generating corporate revenues. Slowly, over time, as those same managers drift further away from customer facing activity, their skills and their sharpness diminish. This becomes a slow and in many cases, silent and imperceptible drain on leadership effectiveness.

How many leaders were promoted into their roles because of their customer-focused expertise, be it sales, technical or operational? And in their new roles, how much of their time and effort is slowly siphoned away from their customer focus, the heart of their value, to internal administrative activities?

What is the impact on the customer? On the company? And on the leader?

To what extent are we reducing valuable, talented leadership assets to the role of glorified administrators? To what extent, in your current role, has your value and impact been marginalized? How much of your time and efforts are devoted to value-added customer focused activities, versus internal administrative activities that could be performed more effectively through other means, or by someone else?

To what extent, even though you may occupy an executive role and an impressive title, have your administrative responsibilities diminished your sales, technical or operational expertise, thus making you less valuable in the marketplace?

The "internal abyss" has the potential to silently drain corporate productivity, rendering companies less competitive in an increasingly competitive marketplace. At the same time, it has the potential to reduce valuable leadership assets to the role of glorified administrators, weakening their competitiveness in the marketplace in the same manner.

Chapter 8

The Opportunity: The Corporation and the "Me" Enterprise

"How can one embrace what is better, when he holds dearly to what is familiar?"

—Ross Kelly

The Art of Letting Go

John Samuelson was seriously considering taking a new position as the Director of Logistics and Warehouse Operations with a major retail distribution company. He had been highly recruited, and the preliminary discussions went well, but he wanted to learn more about the company's operations before making a decision.

The company arranged for John to have a tour of one of the company's largest warehouses. During the tour, he noticed an employee with a handheld scanning device, walking from section to section, scanning shrink-wrapped boxes stacked on pallets 10-15 feet high. He asked the Warehouse Supervisor, "Is he doing inventory? I thought your RFID automation system maintained your inventory."

"It does, Sir," the Warehouse Supervisor replied. "But we use a "belt and suspenders" approach here. You can never be too careful when it comes to inventory."

"How long have you had the RFID? And have you had any issues with accuracy with the technology?" the new Director asked.

"Four years, sir. And we've had no issues with it that I am aware of."

The tour uncovered other similar instances of what, in John's experience, were remnants of business practices and a culture that was not in sync with the type of environment that would allow him to flourish.

John was considered a "go-getter," a "knock down the obstacles and get it done" kind of leader. This did not feel like that type of environment. He respectfully withdrew his name from consideration.

This chapter is about the role of the Corporation in the era of the "Me" Enterprise. It examines the types of companies that have embraced the realities of digitization that are compatible with the "Me" Enterprise. It is about the practices, processes and culture of Corporations that are the ideal partner with the "Me" Enterprise . . . a partner in entrepreneurship and improvements in growth, profitability and productivity.

The "Me" Enterprise is about a set of values, principles and practices exhibited by leaders who consistently find success in the highly competitive digitized workplace. The term encapsulates the characteristics of the best and brightest leaders and emerging leaders and what makes them tick. In Chapter 4, the "Me" Enterprise was defined as:

1. An individual who exhibits excellence in leadership in the digitized, corporate environment of the 21st century.

2. Someone who excels in a corporate environment by applying the attitudes, values, principles and behaviors of a self-employed entrepreneur.

3. An individual whose singular focus is creating, selling and delivering value to their employer or customer.

4. A corporate culture of excellence achieved through results oriented entrepreneurship and individual accountability.

They are confident, self-managed, self-directed, high performing leaders who behave more like entrepreneurs than employees, and aspire to undertake and solve complex problems for their employer. They are on a constant vigil, in search of inefficiencies and problems that can be translated into opportunity. They are leaders who do not look to their employer to be responsible for their success nor their careers. They take responsibility for their own success and take charge of their careers, as if they are their own company. Their attitude, in the vernacular of sports is, "Give me the ball coach." They seek, as one executive described, a work environment that allows them the "freedom to flourish," and in exchange, they deliver high quality results for their company, and themselves.

In turn, what are the practices that successful companies adapt to unburden them from the internal abyss, and at the same time, embrace and leverage the changing conditions brought on by new technologies and increased competition?

How are those companies adjusting their strategies and practices in order to remain competitive in the world of digitization, "uberization" and disruption? What type of organization best suits an individual with the characteristics of the "Me" Enterprise? What is the profile of the company that attracts and retains leaders that embody those attributes? What are their practices? What is their culture? What is it they do better than their competitors to attract the best and the brightest?

What is the corporation's role in fostering and leveraging the benefits of the "Me" Enterprise? How do those corporations engage, embrace and foster the culture and the practices of its leaders who are more entrepreneurial, more self-reliant, and more determined to succeed?

And, most importantly, how are these companies realizing productivity increases of 30, 40 and even 50%, incremental to the benefits of automation or workforce restructuring?

The "Alliance for Productivity:" The Digitized Corporation and the "Me" Enterprise

In our pursuit of answers to these questions, we have had discussions with "C" level executives, mid-level managers and first line supervisors, in companies, large and small, and across all vertical segments, including finance, telecommunications, logistics, manufacturing, service companies and the public sector. We have found a variety of innovative and creative practices that more and more companies are beginning to employ to prosper in today's market conditions. What is outlined below is a collection of practices that represent an alliance for productivity in this world of digitization: The digitized corporation and the "Me" Enterprise.

While some of the practices and trends outlined in this chapter will not come as a surprise, others may seem counter-intuitive. And while we are not so presumptuous as to profess these actions to be the complete, final and absolute set of principles and practices that all companies in all situations should embrace, they represent practices that can create an enhanced alignment between corporations, their leaders and their workforce.

Further, given the complexity and diversity of the subject matter contained in this book, neither do we intend to tell corporate executives how to manage their business, or even recommend how their businesses can be managed more effectively. What we do offer is a collection of findings from a broad cross-section of leaders from a variety of different companies and industries that warrant consideration as emerging "best practices" in the world of digitization.

Additionally, with each we offer our own thoughts and observations and ideas for you to consider . . . thoughts and observations not put forth as a prescription, nor as guidelines, nor or even as recommendations . . . but put forth in the form of questions. Think of them, not to suggest that your company should adapt a particular practice, but to give consideration to the possibilities. Allow yourself to look beyond what is to what could be, and what we believe soon will be.

Think of them in the form of "What if . . . ?"

As you review this collection of practices, thoughts and considerations of "what if," you will find that they tend to fall neatly into four major categories or themes:

1. **Practices that promote a more "entrepreneurial" work environment;**

2. **Practices that promote a more "customer-centric" business model;**

3. **Practices that take an aggressive position on the use of technology;**

4. **Practices that place a strong, "zero tolerance" emphasis on governance and process.**

1. The Entrepreneurial Work Environment

Companies are becoming increasingly entrepreneurial, as are their leaders. Corporate executives are creating an environment of "autonomy with accountability," allowing their teams extended freedom to create and execute business plans, as if they are their own independent company.

Companies are behaving more as holding companies that oversee a portfolio of businesses. The company is the "venture capitalist," and their businesses are the entrepreneurs who are responsible for competing and succeeding in an openly competitive environment. Business unit leaders create and submit business plans; their companies approve or modify those plans, provide the supporting infrastructure, funding and oversight parameters; and the business units execute accordingly, enjoying their autonomy, but fully understanding the accountability that goes with that autonomy.

The mantra, "Lead, follow or get out of the way" is being taken to new levels. Companies are encouraging their leaders to be responsible for their own success, and their leaders are complying.

What if your company . . . created an increasingly entrepreneurial environment in which its leaders and their teams behaved as "start-up's," with the corporation acting as the "Venture Capitalist," that provides funding, support and oversight?

Tom Hansen heads the maintenance division of a regional network and telecommunications company in the southeast U.S. His group is responsible for installation and maintenance of 8,500 commercial and residential network systems around the south.

When he heard that his company was considering outsourcing their installation and maintenance operations to smaller, independent 3rd party providers, Hansen put forth a radical proposal. He asked that, though his group was internal to the company, he be allowed to put forth a bid as an outsourced provider, competing on the same terms related to costs, quality, margins and customer satisfaction, as other outside bidders. The company agreed to his idea, and ultimately determined that Hansen's internal group put forth the most compelling proposal. The company agreed to retain Hansen's internal group based on the condition that the internal group would deliver per its proposal in terms of costs, margins and customer satisfaction. The company agreed to a three-year contract, at which time it would once again put the services contract out for competitive bid.

> "Even though we are in the same company," Hanson said, "I and everyone in our group behave as if we are our own company, providing services on a competitive basis to our parent company. We have to compete every day knowing that we could lose our business at any time to an outside competitor."

What if your company ... set clearer and stronger expectations that their leaders are expected to be responsible for their own careers?

In more and more examples, companies are providing their employees the guidance, direction, tools, training and investments to enable them to succeed, but the company sets no expectations about providing lifetime employment or long-term careers. Consistent with the characteristics and values of the

"Me" Enterprise, companies tend to create an entrepreneurial environment for success, but do not take responsibility for the careers of their employees. Their career guidance tends to consist of the message, "We will provide you the best opportunities and the infrastructure to allow you to succeed in challenging and fulfilling work, but as for your career, it is up to you. You are on your own!"

> "One of the most enduring lessons I learned" recounted a retiring CEO at his farewell banquet, "was when I once asked my boss for career advice. Like the father figure he was to me, he put his hand on my shoulder and politely told me, 'Son, you're on your own.'"
>
> "At the time, I was disappointed and shocked, because I thought he did not care about me and my career. I later learned that he told me that EXACTLY because he cared about me and my career."

What if your company . . . created a stronger culture of individual accountability?

While companies continue to provide the support infrastructure to enable their leaders to succeed (tools, training, processes, etc.), more and more they are giving their managers the same message. Successful companies create a culture that fosters less an "employer/employee" relationship, and more of a "General Contractor/sub-contractor" relationship. Though their leaders are employees in the traditional definition, they are expected to behave and perform as entrepreneurs, as if to say, *"You are on your own."*

What if your company . . . placed an increased emphasis on and promoted the concept of "employability" rather than "employment?"

Relating to companies and their responsibilities to their employees, there is a variation on the axiom, "Give a man a fish and he will eat for a day. Teach a man to fish, and he will eat for a lifetime." The variation is:

> "We cannot offer you lifetime employment; but we can provide you the skills that will make you employable for a lifetime."

In contrast to prior decades and prior circumstances, companies are in no position to promise to prospective employees that they will provide them "full and lasting employment." They are in a position, however, to "create an environment in which you will perform work and develop the skills to effectively compete in this marketplace, thus making you forever employable."

The distinction is subtle, but dramatic. It is a promise to place them in roles that will maximize their talents and expertise, which serves to continually develop and fine-tune their skills, thus making them more desirable and competitive in the marketplace.

What if your company . . . gave its leaders increasing levels of "autonomy with accountability" to unleash and devote their talents to solving interesting, challenging and complex problems?

> "Perhaps the most difficult challenge a leader faces is the willingness to let their leaders lead. I learned that lesson by accident when I got sick and had no choice but to let my managers run things during my absence."
>
> —Steve Jobs

McNeil (Mac) Nelson opened his first men's clothing store in 1967 after dropping out of college. He grew up in the men's clothing business, and felt like he knew what it would take to have a successful retail operation. By 1972, Mac had five stores within a 50-mile radius of his original store. While he continued to manage the original store himself, he promoted employees from his store to manage his other locations.

Having been personally trained by Mac, each of his store managers knew their boss could be characterized as a "control freak." He managed the inventory of each of the stores centrally, with little or no latitude given to his store managers to make buying decisions for their store, even though each of the stores catered to a different demographic.

Within one year after being promoted, two of Mac's store managers left the company, and a third, one that he deemed his best employee, had also given his notice. Having already lost two managers within a year's time, Mac did not want to lose a third, especially his most valuable manager. He requested that the two go to dinner to discuss the situation.

Over dinner, the store manager expressed how much he had learned from Mac, and how much he appreciated the opportunity he had been given. But he felt stifled by Mac's micro-management, and wanted the opportunity to have more control over his store's inventory and advertising. Mac reluctantly agreed to loosen the controls and gave the store manager the freedom to make his own buying and advertising decisions, but also gave him very aggressive revenue and margin targets.

Within the first year of the new agreement, the store manager had not only exceeded the revenue and margin targets Mac had issued, but had also exceeded the revenue and margins of the store that Mac himself managed, which was in a larger market.

"For the first six months, I was as nervous as I could be", Mac recalled. "I was tempted to go down to his store every Monday morning, but my wife told me to leave him alone and let him run his store. He was right, and my wife was right. It's the best decision I ever made, and now I let each of my store managers run their stores the way they believe is best – that is, as long as they deliver!"

Jack Welch once told a group of MBA students, "Sometimes a leader leads best by getting out of the way. Set clear expectations, clear parameters, and clear guidelines, and then let your leaders demonstrate their value and earn their pay. If you trust them, you will let them lead. If you don't trust them, they shouldn't be there in the first place."

2. Customer Focused

Leading corporations are creating practices and establishing roles, responsibilities and practices that ensure that their leaders' primary focus is outward, toward their customers and toward the marketplace, rather than inward. At the core of those practices is the mantra, "EVERYONE in this organization has customer responsibilities."

Even senior leaders, independent of their title or primary responsibilities, retain some direct customer focused responsibilities and accountability for customer performance.

Companies are placing a major emphasis on being externally oriented. They are forging a "customer first" mentality, and aggressively working to eliminate internally oriented practices that impede customer productivity. They aggressively attack activities characterized as "the internal abyss," or any practices that pull leaders away from more productive, customer-facing activities. They find alternative ways to perform the tasks that are deemed essential, and eliminate those that are viewed as menial or unnecessary

What if your company . . . took aggressive actions to eliminate non-value added and redundant administrative tasks, and relieved your customer-facing leaders of unnecessary administrative functions (a.k.a., the "internal abyss")?

The most successful companies tend to be the most dogged in their search to eliminate any administrative activities that get in the way of customer- focused work and production. In many of the examples we reviewed, key questions are asked of every administrative task that consumes time away from the customer. Questions, such as:

- Is this an essential activity?
- How does it make our service to our customer better?
- Is there an automated tool that can eliminate or improve the performance of this task?
- Is there someone else that can perform this task more efficiently?

In more and more cases, companies are employing "administrative specialists" to take on many of the administrative tasks of account teams and other customer facing employees

What if your company . . . transitioned from a "generalist" leadership model to a "specialist" model, in which leaders specialize in either customer-centric functions or administrative functions?

As competitive forces have intensified, companies have increasingly come to appreciate the need to be customer focused, and have instituted a number of practices to do so. However, in the process, many companies simply placed those practices on their leaders, further burdening them with customer-facing "administrative" tasks (i.e., more ceremonial customer visits, more customer reports, etc.). This will have the inverse effect of making their leaders more valuable to their customer, or to the company.

Historically, management roles have been characterized in binary terms of "Line Managers," those with direct revenue, profit and loss responsibilities, such as sales leaders, business unit leaders, etc.; and "Staff" Managers," those who lead support functions, such as Finance, Human Resources, IT and other supporting roles.

Companies are beginning to re-invent that concept, but with a new twist. In the highly competitive world of digitization and knowledge workers, companies are making the distinction between:

- "Content" Leaders (Leaders who have customer facing responsibilities),

    and

- "Administrative" Leaders (those who manage internal administrative functions).

In addition to aggressively reducing management activities that add little or no value, or are redundant, companies are creating the role of administrative specialists and reassigning administrative tasks and responsibilities to those specialists.

In hospitals and health care facilities, for example, doctors and other medical professionals would be considered "content" leaders, while the head of the hospital and the heads of the many support functions in the facility are "administrative" leaders.

What if leaders whose primary expertise was customer-centric work and driving revenue for their company, were relieved of their administrative tasks in order to devote virtually all of their time to revenue-based activities? And what if the administrative tasks were performed by "administrative" leaders, whose domain expertise was in an administrative field, such as finance, human resources or legal?

The Player/Coach

In the specialist model, Content leaders would be responsible for three primary functions:

- Performing customer-centric work,
- Continually learning and mastering their craft, and
- Teaching others on their team.

This approach would allow them to devote a greater portion of their time and effort to customer-oriented work, enhance their proficiency in content related work, and their customer focus would neutralize their cost to the corporation.

Administrative leaders, in turn, would be responsible for the internal, administrative aspects of the business, including employee infrastructure needs, performance inputs, corporate communications and compensation. Administrative leaders provide the staff support to content leaders and their teams, thus enhancing the corporation's efforts toward customer focused work. Additionally, by directing more of a content leader's efforts to revenue-generating activities, the cost of leadership is significantly reduced for the corporation.

Chief Surgeons are elevated up the ranks of the surgical staff within their medical facilities largely by virtue of their surgical expertise, and their leadership qualities. In their leadership role, they typically have two major areas of responsibility:

1. They continue to perform surgical procedures, and

2. They perform a leadership role in guiding and overseeing the quality and state of the art of surgical staff within their facility.

Medical facilities realize that the fundamental value of the Chief Surgeon and the entire surgical staff is in their ability to perform high quality surgical procedures. And they realize that the more surgical procedures they perform, the greater their expertise and individual value, and the greater their value to their hospital.

As a result, hospitals take extraordinary measures to limit the amount of administrative work or other non-value added tasks to the workload of their surgical staff. Those tasks are generally assigned to administrative specialists, who develop comparable levels of expertise within their respective administrative domains.

The results are threefold:

1. The surgical staff is able to eliminate non-value added tasks to their workday, thus positioning them to devote their time and effort to those activities that achieve the greatest value for their corporations;

2. The surgical staff is able to concentrate their efforts on sharpening their skills and knowledge within their respective domains, thus enhancing their career value;

3. Likewise, Administrators develop comparable expertise and domain knowledge within their administrative domains, enhancing their value to the corporation, and their career value.

Leading consulting firms adhere to a similar model. Their consulting teams are led by what many call "Managing Principals," who serve as team leaders on the firm's larger, more complex engagements. Managing Principals typically are promoted from the ranks of the organization by virtue of their expertise in securing and executing client engagements, and, like Chief Surgeons in a hospital, they have two major areas of responsibility:

1. They continue to direct and oversee consulting engagements, where they continue to perform billable client work, and

2. They lead and oversee the quality and execution of other consulting teams.

In each of these examples, both the Chief Surgeon in the hospital and the Managing Principal in the consulting firm have minimal administrative responsibilities, thus allowing them to give maximum value and productivity to their customer/patient-oriented activities. This structure enables them to concentrate on delivering a service to their clients and financial value to their respective organizations, and to rely on "Administrative leaders" to provide the administrative support and expertise in areas such as Human Resources, Finance, Legal and IT.

Just as the value of the Chief Surgeon and Managing Principal is maximized by allowing them to concentrate on their customer oriented activities, so is the value of HR, Finance and IT leaders who are specialists in their own rights. By specializing in their respective fields, they are able to provide higher levels of expertise for their administrative activities, which are equally critical to the performance of the corporation.

In examining successful corporations today, there is a direct correlation between those corporations whose leaders have direct customer-based responsibilities, and the revenue, margin and customer satisfaction levels those organizations achieve. What if more corporations adopted the model of a Chief Surgeon in a hospital, or a Managing Principal in a leading consulting firm? What if organizations applied a similar leadership model in which leaders specialized in either a customer-focused domain, or an administrative domain?

How would a "specialist" leadership model impact productivity in contrast to the more "generalist" model that most corporations employ today? How would a specialist model enhance the expertise of its leaders? What if leaders concentrated on and specialized in a particular domain? How much deeper would their content knowledge go? How much more value and productivity would they bring to their corporation, and to their own expertise and value in their corporate effectiveness?

What would it look like if a corporate division of 100 employees transitioned from a generalist to a specialist leadership model?

In the generalist model, the team of 100 workers is organized into 10 teams, each consisting of a General Manager who oversees all management and leadership functions for the group, and ten team leaders, who assume the same management and leadership functions for their team. In that model, there are eleven "General Managers," each performing both customer related and administrative management functions, and eighty-nine workers.

In the specialist model, there is one General Manager and two "Group Leaders" who perform the administrative functions for their group. The Group Leader role is somewhat of a hybrid role that "harmonizes" the balance between "content" issues and "administrative" issues. The teams are now organized into eight teams of 12 members each, and led by Player/Coaches, who in addition to their coaching roles, also have customer-facing responsibilities. This model fosters greater levels of expertise, and provides a total of ninety-seven customer facing experts.

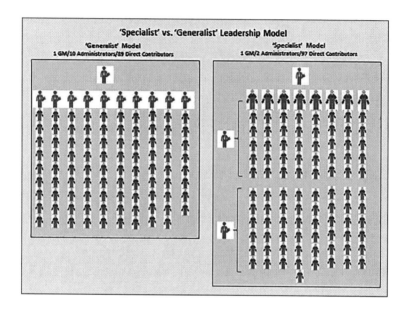

If we were to apply a "purity" test to this axiom, "content" leaders would not perform any administrative tasks; and "administrative" leaders would not perform any content-related tasks. But since hospitals, as well as other corporations, are far from pure in the practical delineation of roles and responsibilities, we do not believe in, nor are we advocating a purist approach to this model. What we are seeing is a modified, pragmatic variation which employs the following principles:

1. While "Content" Leaders, for all practical purposes, cannot be and should not be completely exempt from administrative tasks, the administrative

responsibilities they perform should be held to an absolute minimum, in order to gain their maximum productivity, and should be performed primarily by administrative staff.

2. While "Administrative" Leaders should be responsible for primarily performing administrative tasks, it is also recognized that Administrative leaders possess valuable expertise, which can and should be leveraged in direct support of the corporation's business.

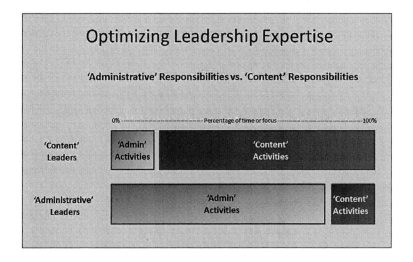

Both Content leaders and Administrative leaders have valuable and mission critical expertise, and each should have responsibilities in each domain. In order to realize incremental productivity gains, however, those responsibilities should be finely tuned to their core function and to the value they bring to their corporate entities.

In support of their customer focus, companies should

ensure that their leaders continue to develop, sustain and enhance their technical or domain skills, even as they advance up the corporate ladder. This practice is intended to foster and re-enforce domain expertise, either in a customer facing domain, or in an administrative domain. Leaders who were once technical specialists in their earlier individual contributor days, are positioned to retain and continue to practice their technical specialty, even though they are now leaders. Rather than lose their specialization when promoted into leadership positions, they continue to practice as "player/coaches," leading and training others, as they continue as a practitioner.

3. Technology Fanatics

It is hardly a surprise that, in the era of digitization, leading companies are those that are aggressively pursuing, embracing and adopting new technologies. These are companies that do not fear the onslaught of new and disruptive technologies; they throw themselves at it. These are companies that commit themselves not to be the "disruptee," but the "disruptor" of new practices and new business models conceived by new technologies.

Whether it is a technology company, a services company, a government enterprise, or a local retail outlet, technology has become a major part of the DNA of business. And leading corporations relish that reality.

What if your company . . . was fanatical about pursuing and adopting new technologies?

After experiencing wave after wave of new technologies, new applications, and new innovations, companies are beginning to realize that they were being overwhelmed with the constant barrage, and need to create a more "forward leaning" approach to the process of assessing and instituting new technologies.

Stan Michaels is the founder and CEO of a data analytics firm that, by its very nature, is in the eye of the hurricane of new technologies.

> Our core business is about technology. And you will never find a CEO that is as aggressive about technology as I am. But it seemed like at every Monday morning staff meeting, someone was introducing the newest technology, the latest, greatest application. The meetings began to turn into an academic debate about what was good and what was bad, and I felt like we were just drowning in new technologies with no rhyme or reason as to what to use, and what not to use. So, I decided to form what I called the "Sandbox team." They were a group that would be responsible for researching, analyzing and bringing recommendations for new technologies to our leadership team. We created what we felt would be an organized, pro-active approach to get in front of the constant waves we were being hit with.

Every company, in or outside of the eye of the hurricane of new technologies, is impacted by those technologies and must compete in an environment that becomes more dependent on technology every day. As Stan Michaels said, "Get in front of it, or get run over by it!"

What if your company . . . made technical fluency a major selection factor in hiring and promotion practices, including for its most senior leadership positions?

As an adjunct axiom to the previous recommendation,

"Technology has become pervasive, and NO ONE, no matter what their job is, should be immune.

P.V. Rau is the founder and CEO of a California-based company that provided network components to telecommunications providers. As a technologist who headed a technology company, Rau was determined that all employees in his company should have a "fluency" in technology. He embarked on a series of mandatory "lunch and learn" sessions in which his employees would receive training, not just on all of his company's products and technologies, but technology in general. He called the series, "The Technology Universe."

Very proud of the reception of the lunch and learn series, he decided to introduce a similar session at his next board meeting. During the session, he and his Board members both realized that his Board was, by comparison to company employees, in the Dark Ages in their knowledge about some of the very basic aspects of telecommunications technologies and technology in general. They further realized that his Board was largely made up of successful academics and business leaders, but had no representation from the more technically savvy "Millennial" segment. In addition to continuing the "lunch and learn" sessions with his Board, he and the Board agreed that they needed to add another position to the Board in support of their agreed strategy that, EVERYONE, including Board members, needed to be technically fluent.

What is the technical fluency of your company? If it is lingering in the "dark ages," time is of the essence. Perhaps a "lunch and learn" or other learning process is in order to get everyone into the realm of technology and its coming trends.

What if your company . . . employed assertive business practices, aided by the aggressive use of Enterprise Resource Planning (ERP), Customer Relationship Management (CRM)

**and related technologies, to eliminate the productivity gap
and create permanency in the transient times that typically
occur during leadership transitions?**

Historically, employees worked for the same leader on
average from 18 months to two years. The issue of transitioning
from one leader to another, or from one division to another was
not a significant drag on productivity. Today, those transitions
occur on the average of every 6-8 months. Transition times are
times of lost productivity, unless aggressive actions are taken to
eliminate them.

James Twohey made a major career decision, resigning from
his position as a Sales Engineer for a chemical supply company,
to become a Senior Account Executive for a competitor, where
he would be calling on Fortune 50 accounts.

After enjoying a two-week vacation, James arrived for
his first day on the new job, which consisted of a non-stop
marathon of orientation sessions with his new company, from
Human Resources, to IT, to Legal, to Administrative Services.
His final appointment of the day was with his new boss, the
VP of Sales and Marketing, who provided James with a new
laptop computer, already loaded with the company's customer
relationship management (CRM) application, fully populated
with detailed history of client contacts and activities, pipeline
status and the current quarterly forecast for each client. The end
of the quarter was less than one month away.

His boss also arranged a video conference with James' new
team, allowing each sales representative to introduce themselves
and provide a status update on their respective pipelines, and
actions required to close current opportunities by end-of-
quarter.

Following the call, using the CRM application, his new boss
reviewed the information they had just heard on the call, and
concluded with his expected actions and results for James to

close out the current quarter, as had been forecast and reported by his new team.

Following his meeting with his new boss, James concluded his day on the phone with the company's travel agent, creating a week long travel itinerary which would begin the following morning.

Finally home after a long and grueling first day on the new job, when asked by his new wife how it went, James said, "If I thought I was going to be able to ease in to this new job with a honeymoon period, I was sadly mistaken. They expect me to deliver results for this quarter, like I've been here for six months! I have to go upstairs and pack."

ERP, CRM, Electronic Medical Records and other related technologies have given companies the ability to ease the disruption of transitions and reduce down time in dramatic fashion. The companies that aggressively take advantage of these technologies have also established a culture of expectation that productivity begins on Day One!

When the CEO of an electronics re-seller was asked about "honeymoon periods for new employees, he said, "Every day of a honeymoon period is a day lost to the competition."

4. "Zero Tolerance" Governance Policies

"We all will suffer one of two things: the pain of discipline, or the pain of failure."

—Jim Rohn

The three cornerstones of any corporation are typically regarded as people, technology and process. Of the three, process serves as the bridge between people and technology, and is typically coupled with another term, "governance."

Governance covers a broad range of corporate activities. From routine adherence to processes and procedures, to compliance with Federal and International laws, governance is the foundation of an organization's culture, and has proven to have a direct correlation to corporate success.

Governance, however, is viewed by many managers as a necessary evil, a distraction that gets in the way of the "real work" they have to do. It is sometimes demeaned as unimportant and given the term "administrivia" . . . which means trivial, bureaucratic and that which adds little or no value to the company's business performance. While the perception is real, and most likely born from an improper application of governance practices, as opposed to the critical nature and intent of those practices, the characterization could not be further from the true nature of its importance.

One misapplication of governance practices, and one that is on the increase due to the increase in analytics technologies, is in the area of performance metrics. There is an expression that "metrics drives behavior." In other words, what a leader or an employee is measured on and how they are measured, dictates what they do and how they do it. So, what is the potential misapplication of metrics? In short . . . they are too many and too complex.

As a leading energy management firm instituted a new ERP/sales management system, the executive team discovered a wide range of new performance indicators that the software could monitor in the area of sales performance. Prior to implementing the new system, the metrics for sales teams were simple and straightforward:

> . . . # of leads generated,
> . . . # of proposals delivered,
> . . . # of proposals closed, and
> . . . amount of revenue generated.

The new software provided insights into a much broader range of sales activities, such as the number of sales calls, the number of customer visits, the number of customer social events, and the costs associated with each of these activities.

Armed with this new intelligence, the performance metrics for sales leaders and sales representatives were expanded to include each of these newly discovered performance indicators. Further, sales compensation was modified to incentivize performance against the new indicators. Sales representatives, for example, were given bonuses for exceeding the monthly thresholds for the number of customer visits and the number of sales calls. Likewise, bonuses were withheld if they did not achieve their targets for visits and sales calls.

The company had fallen into what has come to be characterized as the "metrics mania trap." What the company did not realize or appreciate is the distinction between "metrics," which are intended to be simple and straightforward, and "analytics," which entail a much more detailed diagnosis of performance.

Performance indicators provided by analytics technologies and metrics and compensation systems should complement one another, but should not be merged to become one singular process.

What if your company ... resisted metrics mania and adhered to the basic principles of performance metrics: "Simple, not complex;" "Less is more;" and what if they made a clean distinction between "metrics" and "analytics?"

A corollary to the "metrics mania" trap is the newly appointed manager who wants to bring in his or her own system of managing and measuring.

Anthony Kirkland, when hired by a third party logistics provider, was deemed to be a highly successful process engineering manager. He described himself to his new company as a "techno-geek," and also a self-proclaimed master of analytics. He was viewed by his new employer as the prototypical "manager of the future" in the fast moving world of logistics and shipping. Kirkland was the third new logistics manager in as many years when he assumed his role with his new company, and believed he had been hired to bring in his "system" to turn around the new company's warehouse and shipping operations.

As in the previous example, Kirkland too, introduced a new and much more complicated system of measures and controls which required new software systems and extensive training for all his employees to learn the new system.

Kirkland, also as in the previous example, combined metrics, which is designed to focus on results, with analytical "performance indicator" data, which places more emphasis on process improvement and efficiency, thus creating an overly complex system of metrics.

The resistance to "metrics mania" includes the resistance of providing every new manager who comes into the company with an improved scheme to add what he or she may perceive to be a new and better metrics system.

A second corollary to the "metrics mania" trap is how compensation is tied to performance metrics. In an effort to incentivize employees to perform certain activities, there is the potential to (1) provide incentives for "activities" rather than results, and (2) to run the risk of inadvertently motivating employees to compromise ethical behaviors.

The same sales team referenced in the previous example was given a new set of metrics criteria that would govern their quarterly and annual bonuses. One metric, for example, was the number of sales "socials" they conducted, events designed to create an informal social setting where business could be transacted. Based on the number of sales social events they were expected to achieve in a given quarter, their bonus was withheld if they failed to deliver the prescribed number of events, and was issued if they exceeded the number of events.

In discussions with the sales leader, who by the way, had no input in the revised metrics and compensation plan, it was revealed that if they were short of social visits, sales representatives would simply invite a customer out for dinner and drinks, and declare the evening a sales social event.

Whereas the previous sales metrics and compensation systems were simple, straightforward and effective, the company was lured by its new technologies into a more complicated process of measuring and compensating sales activities as well as results. The new metrics and compensation systems were both manipulated to achieve the desired management optics and the desired outcome and bonus for the sales representative; but they did nothing to achieve the outcome management had intended. The practice further encouraged similar "work arounds" on other performance indicators that the sales teams felt were meaningless in the actual process of delivering results.

Technology brings with it the risk of adding unnecessary complexity, if misapplied, and in the process, it can increase the potential to add confusion rather than effectiveness in improving performance. In this case, the introduction of a new system and a new set of assumptions, instead of enhancing the sales function and its results, diluted not only the effectiveness, but also the integrity of the sales management process.

What if your company . . . ensured that compensation systems did not create the unintended consequence of encouraging policy or ethical violations for the purpose of enhancing personal compensation; and metrics and related compensation targets were focused on customer outcomes, not structured in ways that could lead to compromises or transgressions of ethics, policies or procedures?

A third dimension of governance pertains to process and data reporting.

Using the example cited in the previous chapter in which consultants were required to complete weekly Labor Activity Reports (LARs), a reporting system which shaped hiring and staffing decisions, we learned that the strong emphasis on the timing of the reports had the unintended consequence of compromising the quality of reports.

Given the major emphasis placed on consultants completing the reports at the end of each week, the quality of the data was deeply flawed, and required an almost completely redundant manual quality check of the information provided. At a broader level, given the redundancy of both the automated and manual oversight process, the expense of the reporting system and the time and effort required to complete and analyze the reports was largely wasted money and effort.

One of the adjustments in the system made in this particular example was the time at which reports were completed and submitted. The weekly reports were eliminated and a new process was designed where the LAR reports could be completed by the consultants on an engagement basis. In fact, the system was designed so that consultants couldn't proceed to the next assignment without completing a report on current engagements.

This new system resulted in a more timely and accurate report.

What was initially perceived to be a flawed system was in actuality a flawed design. How the reports were compiled and who compiled the reports and consolidated them for management consumption was the real culprit. Once the design was reconfigured, the quality and integrity of the data improved dramatically, and eventually the need for redundant oversight was eliminated as well.

What if your company . . . designed and implemented reporting processes based on the quality and integrity of the data, and not on artificial deadlines? And what if reports were completed on an engagement basis, rather than creating composite reports weekly or monthly, via use of the reporting mantra: "Clean, timely, useful information, without redundant effort?"

> "Compliance with effective processes equals
> successful results."

Though it is on many occasions invisible to the uneducated eye, there is a growing correlation between compliance with governance and process, and achieving results. More and more companies are discovering this correlation, and accordingly, they are instituting strict, "zero tolerance" approaches to ensure that all employees adhere to their processes and procedures . . . from routine processes, to ethical behaviors, to corporate policy, to government laws and regulations.

To emphasize their focus on compliance, many companies have instituted internal audit or oversight committees whose responsibilities are to ensure proper compliance with corporate policies and procedures, while at the same time constantly examining the quality of processes to ensure quality outputs and eliminate redundant, unnecessary steps in the process.

Further, these companies are taking steps to train and certify their managers in governance practices, holding them directly accountable for process and quality management. In these companies, they do not rely on auditors to uncover issues of non-compliance or ethical violations. Their managers, at all levels, are accountable as the first line of defense in corporate compliance and governance issues, from day-to-day policies and procedures, to compliance with "best practices," to financial controls and local and federal government regulations and laws.

What if your company . . . required its leaders to be trained and certified in process and management controls, and made them accountable as the first line of defense in governance compliance, and further enacted "zero tolerance" policies related to governance?

What if your company . . . subject to size and scalability, instituted an internal audit or "Quality" office to guide and oversee the creation and compliance with best practices, policies, procedures and guidelines?

* * *

"What if . . ." A simple, innocuous question which has the potential to uncover questions unanswered and solutions unsolved. In this case, applied to these and other ideas, it has the potential to unleash the undiscovered power and imagination of companies and their employees to be more competitive, more profitable, and better prepared for what has yet to come.

In conclusion . . .

Corporations have been forced to make significant and in some cases, dramatic changes in light of the increasing competitive and financial pressures driven by new technologies, globalization and financial downturns. Those changes, in turn, have served as the impetus for the creation of the "Me" Enterprise, where employees have begun to act more like entrepreneurs than employees, aggressively pursuing challenging opportunities and taking charge of their own careers.

In parallel, companies are doing the same. Those that are successfully navigating their way through the perils, challenges and opportunities brought forth by digitization are doing so, more and more, with the attitudes, practices and culture of entrepreneurship.

The result: For those who have embraced these principles, the dissonance that both employer and employee have experienced in this age of disruption can once again give way to harmony. The digitized corporation and the "Me" Enterprise are emerging as the perfect alliance in the workplace of the 21st century.

Epilogue

Change (n): An endless series of actions and reactions created by disruptive innovations, resulting in a perpetual state of disharmony.

Change Management (n): The endless pursuit of harmony.

THE CYCLES OF change continue . . . a series of disruptive actions, triggered by innovation and resulting in a state of disharmony, followed by reactions, in an effort to regain that harmony; only to do it again, and again, and again. . . .

That cycle is embedded in the fabric of our lives, and certainly in the fabric of corporations. Only now, it occurs at warp speed. The cycles of harmony, to disharmony, back to harmony, which used to happen in timeframes of years and months, now happen in months and weeks.

The dot.com boom was a major disruptive force. The technological innovations that emerged in the 1990s, exacerbated by globalization and economic downturns, triggered an unprecedented phase of disharmony between corporations and their workforce. Corporations were forced to adopt new technologies, create new business practices, new ways of competing in a global economy, and to cut costs, all out of the necessity to survive. Their workforce paid the price. Not since the Industrial Revolution have companies had to confront the harsh prospects of extinction more than in the past quarter century. Businesses, with all good intentions, were caught in a fight for survival, and were no longer able to sustain the nurturing, paternalistic employment practices of previous decades.

With safeguards of a benevolent corporation no longer in place, employees found themselves thrust into a paradigm of "You are on your own." Whatever feelings of harmony that may have existed between employer and employee prior to the heyday of the technology revolution of the 1990s, were gone. The decade of the 2000s and into the 2010s marked a major turning point in the way businesses operated, and in turn, the way employees are being forced to respond.

Increasingly, employees, supervisors, managers and leaders at all levels, have found themselves at risk and ill prepared to survive and/or thrive in their careers. But in response, like their employers who were forced to innovate as a result of change, so have many employees, supervisors, managers and leaders.

The emergence of the "Me" Enterprise is the response to this new reality. The "Me" Enterprise is the antidote, a harmonious counterbalance to what has been, both for companies and their employees, a very disharmonious period.

The "Me" Enterprise provides a mindset, a set of disciplines, and the means from which employees and leaders at all levels can not only survive the treacherous and unpredictable seas of the digitized economy, but even thrive.

The Blueprint of the "Me" Enterprise provides a systematic and organized approach to being prepared for the inevitable uncertainties that await corporations, and more importantly, their employees. Followed with discipline and determination, this blueprint yields the readiness and the self-confidence to undertake any and all eventualities in a turbulent, yet exciting world.

The "Me" Enterprise . . .

1. An individual who exhibits excellence in leadership in the digitized, corporate environment of the 21st century.

2. Someone who excels in a corporate environment by applying the attitudes, values, principles and behaviors of a self-employed entrepreneur.

3. An individual whose singular focus is creating, selling and delivering value to their employer or customer.

4. A corporate culture of excellence achieved through results-oriented entrepreneurship and individual accountability.

. . . an enterprise of one is no longer dependent on their employer, but an interdependent partner with their employer. The "Me" Enterprise is the source of harmony between employer and employee in an otherwise disharmonious environment.

If you are new to the "Me" Enterprise, as with any startup venture, getting started requires planning and effort. But once off the ground, most of the subsequent efforts can be performed while in your current position.

Also, as with any new enterprise, you should begin with your mission. The formula for your mission, M= PC2, to expand your capabilities, multiplied by positioning and promoting those capabilities through an ever-growing network of connections, is a powerful foundation, not for "employment," but for a lifetime of "employability."

The intent of this book has been to raise awareness of the profound impact the phenomenon of digitization, uberization and disruption has had on employees and employers alike. But its primary purpose is to create in you, acting as your own enterprise, a constructive dissatisfaction, knowing that the next change, the next disruption, the next uberization, is coming sooner rather than later, and serving as your call to action, to get started on planning and investing in your "Me" Enterprise.

So, in the classic style of consultants, we bid you adieu . . . not with a prescription, not with guidelines, not even with recommendations . . . but with questions . . . questions that we believe, when answered, can result in greater harmony between employer and employee, and in an increased likelihood of survival in the 21st century . . . the age of digitization.

End

About the Book

As new and disruptive technologies continue to transform the workplace, both employers and employees struggle to keep pace. The business practices of even five years ago are being revamped by new technologies, new applications, new devices, and new modes of connectivity and analytics, leaving many corporations out of touch, out of date and in some cases, out of business. As corporations scramble to keep pace, by way of downsizing, mergers, acquisitions, outsourcing, re-organizations and re-structuring, employees have been left to their own devices to find their niche in a new, increasingly competitive, digitized workplace.

Am I at risk?

How much of your conversations with friends, colleagues and bosses involve talk of mergers, acquisitions, downsizing, re-organizations, outsourcing, or other types of corporate re-structuring? How much of your thought process is consumed by the possibilities that, despite your performance, your job could go away? Today's workforce faces unprecedented employment risks . . . not because of performance issues, or due to a sinking economy, but because of the rapid introduction of new technologies and new levels of competition.

Am I prepared?

Do I have the skills to compete in an economy and work environment that is in a state of constant change? Would I be competitive in the open job market? I was clearly marketable three years ago; but what about today? Have things changed right before my eyes without me noticing it, leaving me ill prepared for what may come next with my company? Do I have the connections to help me make a change if that were necessary? What would happen if I lost my job tomorrow?

"The Emergence of the "Me" Enterprise" provides a historical and analytical view of how digitization has disrupted the workplace, and outlines a set of practices and values, described as the *"Me Enterprise Blueprint,"* which serves as a recipe for surviving and thriving in this "you are on your own" environment.

About the Authors

Ashok Shah

After retiring from Alcatel-Lucent as President of their Global Professional Services organization, Ashok Shah spends his time serving as an advisor or as a member of the Board of Directors for a collection of public and private businesses and universities. He is the founder and President of CEPS Consulting LLC, based in Warren NJ.

G. Ross Kelly

Following his retirement as Vice President of Sales and Consulting Services from Hewlett Packard's Services Division, Ross Kelly embarked on a second career assisting and advising start-up companies and entrepreneurs. Additionally, in support of his passions as a writer, musician and songwriter, he founded a non-profit, EmmaSaid Productions LLC, which provides assistance to aspiring authors and songwriters.

To contact the authors. . . .

Ashok Shah – ashokshah@ceps-consulting.com
Ross Kelly – rosskelly426@gmail.com